Female California
sea lion

Male walrus

Eyewitness
WHALE

Written by
VASSILI PAPASTAVROU

Photographed by
FRANK GREENAWAY

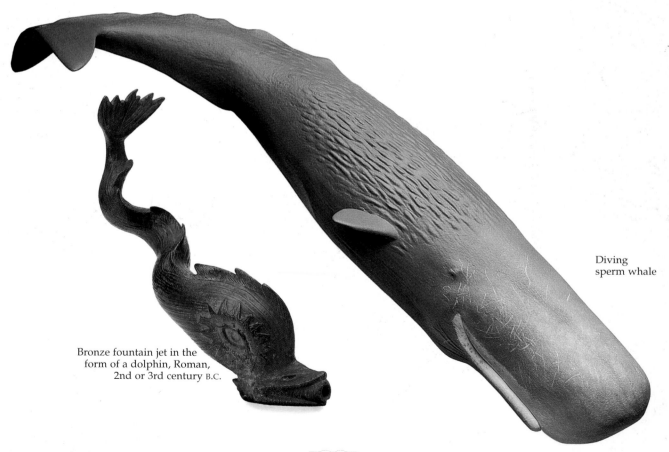

Diving
sperm whale

Bronze fountain jet in the
form of a dolphin, Roman,
2nd or 3rd century B.C.

Dorling Kindersley

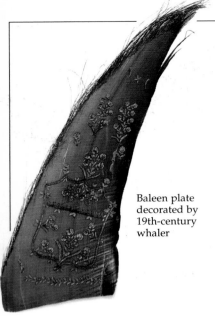

Baleen plate decorated by 19th-century whaler

Upper jaw of extinct whale *Basilosaurus*

Sperm whale tooth scrimshaw

DK

LONDON, NEW YORK, MUNICH, MELBOURNE, and DELHI

Project editor Scott Steedman
Art editor Bob Gordon
Managing editor Helen Parker
Managing art editor Julia Harris
Researcher Céline Carez
Picture research Sarah Moule
Production Catherine Semark
Live animals photographed at Marineland, Antibes, France
and Harderwijk Marine Mammal Park, Holland
Editorial consultants Dr Peter Evans and
Dr Paul Thompson

PAPERBACK EDITION
Managing editor Andrew Macintyre
Managing art editor Jane Thomas
Editor and reference compiler Francesca Baines
Art editor Catherine Goldsmith
Production Jenny Jacoby
Picture research Jo Haddon
DTP designer Siu Ho

This Eyewitness ® Guide has been conceived by
Dorling Kindersley Limited and Editions Gallimard

Hardback edition first published in Great Britain in 1993.
This edition published in Great Britain in 2002
by Dorling Kindersley Limited,
80 Strand, London WC2R ORL

A CIP catalogue record for this book is
available from the British Library.

ISBN 0 7513 4753 1

Colour reproduction by
Colourscan, Singapore
Printed in Hong Kong by Toppan

See our complete
catalogue at

www.dk.com

Whale meal

Spermaceti oil

Dyed baleen bristles

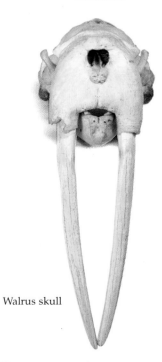

Walrus skull

Narwhal skull with long tusk

Eyewitness
WHALE

3

The Dionysus Cup,
ancient Greek, c. 540 B.C.

Krill

Roman coin with
boy riding dolphin,
2nd century B.C.

17th-century engraving of whales
and whaling

Ancient Greek
bone figure of dolphin
with coral eye

Leaping killer
whale, or orca

Common dolphin

Dolphin-shaped
faience vase
from Rhodes,
550–500 B.C.

Gray whale

Contents

Marine mammals

AT FIRST SIGHT A DOLPHIN looks more like a fish than a person. But like you, the dolphin is a mammal, a warm-blooded animal that feeds its young on mother's milk. It is one of the many kinds of whale, the most successful group of marine mammals. Several other unrelated groups of mammals, including seals and dugongs, also make their homes in salt water. Millions of years ago their ancestors left the land to live in the sea. Over time they evolved to suit their new environment, becoming sleek and streamlined. Unlike fish, which take oxygen from the water, marine mammals must come to the surface regularly to breathe. But taking oxygen from the air is efficient, and most marine mammals are fast swimmers and powerful hunters.

ARISTOTLE
Whales are mammals, not fish. The Greek scientist and philosopher Aristotle recognized this 2,400 years ago. He also noticed that they suckle their young and breathe air, like other mammals.

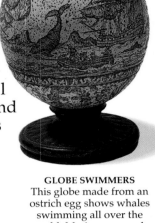

GLOBE SWIMMERS
This globe made from an ostrich egg shows whales swimming all over the world. Marine mammals live in every ocean, from the balmy tropics to the icy polar seas, and in several great rivers. Some migrate vast distances to feed and give birth.

WHALE SIZED
In every language, whale means "big"! Even the smallest whales are the size of a person. This pilot whale weighs 1,300 kg (2,850 lb), about 18 times more than an adult man. The largest whales are bigger than any dinosaur and the blue whale, the largest of all, weighs 200 tonnes and is as long as a Boeing 737 jet!

Layer of fur protects and keeps animal warm

FIN FOOT
Seals, sea lions, and walruses are all pinnipeds, which means "fin footed". They are powerful swimmers superbly adapted to life in the sea. As their name suggests, they have webbed feet. But unlike whales, they have not lost their back legs and have to come ashore to give birth.

Powerful front flippers used to propel sea lion through water

SEA MONSTER
Whales are mysterious creatures. The biggest species live far out to sea and spend most of their lives under water. Early drawings were based on sailors' stories of sea monsters with huge mouths that huffed and puffed like dragons.

Webbed back flippers

Dorsal fin

Blow-hole

WHALES AND DOLPHINS
Of all marine mammals, the best adapted to life in the sea are the cetaceans, or whales. The group gets its name from the Greek word _ketos_, meaning "sea monster". It includes dolphins and porpoises, which are really whales. This bottlenose dolphin is a typical whale. It is a powerful swimmer with strong tail flukes, two pectoral (chest) fins, a dorsal (back) fin, and no hind legs. It breathes through a blow-hole on the top of its head.

Pectoral fins, used to steer while swimming

Tough, rubbery skin with very few hairs

Swimming muscles that drive the whale through water

Flukes, the correct name for a whale's "tail"

THAR SHE BLOWS!
No group of animals has been hunted as ruthlessly as whales (pp. 46–51). They were once common in all the world's oceans, but by the middle of this century many populations had been virtually wiped out. The industry declined, and a public outcry helped to control the killing. But many whale populations may never recover (p. 63).

SEA SIRENS
Like whales, manatees and dugongs have no hind legs and spend their entire lives in the water (pp. 44–45). They are gentle vegetarians, and sailors used to mistake them for mermaids. They are known as sirenians, from the Greek word for mermaid, _seiren_.

Light colour blends in with snow and ice of Arctic

SEA BEAR
Are polar bears marine mammals? Probably, because they depend on the sea. For much of the year, polar bears live on the floating ice pack. Hunting on the ice they ambush seals by air holes. They are superb swimmers but cannot stay under water very long.

Heavy coat of fur keeps bear warm

Powerful paws used to kill prey such as seals

SEA OTTER
Most otters are found in rivers, but there are two species that live all the time in salt water. Sea otters entered the oceans relatively recently and are not as well adapted as other marine mammals. They are sleek and streamlined, with dense fur and webbed feet.

Whale evolution

THE FIRST MAMMALS all lived on land. How or why the ancestors of whales returned to the sea is still unclear. About 55 million years ago, a group of mammals seem to have colonized salty estuaries teeming with fish. Over the millennia, they gradually changed to suit their watery home. Skulls of early whales show how their nostrils moved to the top of the head to make breathing under water easier. Strong tail flukes for swimming evolved, front limbs turned into blades for steering, and back limbs slowly wasted away. Baleen whales have developed a different way of feeding (pp. 24–25), but they probably share the same ancestors as toothed whales. One clue is that they are born with tiny tooth buds that never develop.

AN EARLY WHALE?
Most scientists agree that whales have the same ancestors as even-toed ungulates (hoofed animals), which include modern cows and deer. These ancestors lived on land and hunted other animals. This is a model of *Mesonyx*, an odd carnivore that looked like a wolf but had hooves like a cow. Just like today's carnivores, *Mesonyx* had several different kinds of teeth (pp. 22–23).

OLD WHALE
The *archæocetes* (Latin for old whales) lived in shallow seas and salty estuaries 55 million years ago. Their nostrils were still at the front of their heads.

Nostrils near front of snout

Variety of teeth, like a modern land mammal

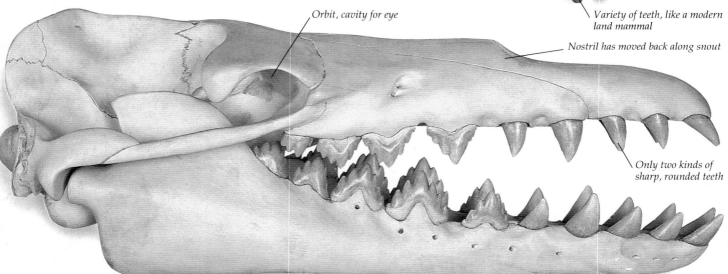

Orbit, cavity for eye

Nostril has moved back along snout

Only two kinds of sharp, rounded teeth

SEAFOOD PLATTER
We know almost nothing about how early whales lived. But the teeth give some clues. *Prozeuglodon isis* probably lived in shallow water, where it caught fish and ground up shells to eat the soft-bodied animals within.

MORE LIKE A DOLPHIN
In some ways the skull of *Prosqualodon davidi*, which lived 25 million years ago, looks like a modern dolphin's skull (p. 23). Its blow-hole must have been near the top of its head, and its teeth are all a similar size and shape.

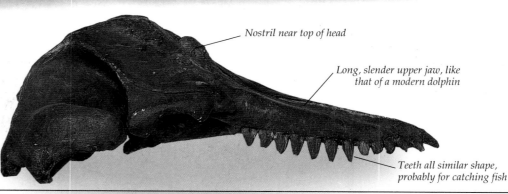

Nostril near top of head

Long, slender upper jaw, like that of a modern dolphin

Teeth all similar shape, probably for catching fish

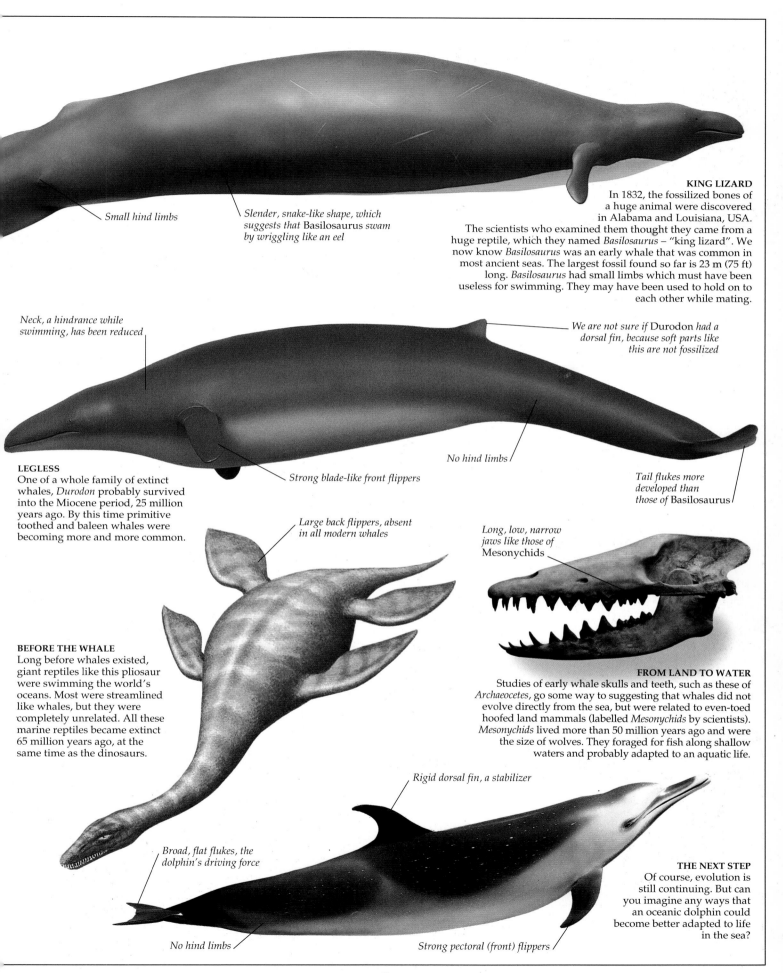

Small hind limbs

Slender, snake-like shape, which suggests that Basilosaurus _swam by wriggling like an eel_

KING LIZARD
In 1832, the fossilized bones of a huge animal were discovered in Alabama and Louisiana, USA. The scientists who examined them thought they came from a huge reptile, which they named _Basilosaurus_ – "king lizard". We now know _Basilosaurus_ was an early whale that was common in most ancient seas. The largest fossil found so far is 23 m (75 ft) long. _Basilosaurus_ had small limbs which must have been useless for swimming. They may have been used to hold on to each other while mating.

Neck, a hindrance while swimming, has been reduced

We are not sure if Durodon _had a dorsal fin, because soft parts like this are not fossilized_

LEGLESS
One of a whole family of extinct whales, _Durodon_ probably survived into the Miocene period, 25 million years ago. By this time primitive toothed and baleen whales were becoming more and more common.

Strong blade-like front flippers

No hind limbs

Tail flukes more developed than those of Basilosaurus

Large back flippers, absent in all modern whales

Long, low, narrow jaws like those of Mesonychids

BEFORE THE WHALE
Long before whales existed, giant reptiles like this pliosaur were swimming the world's oceans. Most were streamlined like whales, but they were completely unrelated. All these marine reptiles became extinct 65 million years ago, at the same time as the dinosaurs.

FROM LAND TO WATER
Studies of early whale skulls and teeth, such as these of _Archaeocetes_, go some way to suggesting that whales did not evolve directly from the sea, but were related to even-toed hoofed land mammals (labelled _Mesonychids_ by scientists). _Mesonychids_ lived more than 50 million years ago and were the size of wolves. They foraged for fish along shallow waters and probably adapted to an aquatic life.

Rigid dorsal fin, a stabilizer

Broad, flat flukes, the dolphin's driving force

THE NEXT STEP
Of course, evolution is still continuing. But can you imagine any ways that an oceanic dolphin could become better adapted to life in the sea?

No hind limbs

Strong pectoral (front) flippers

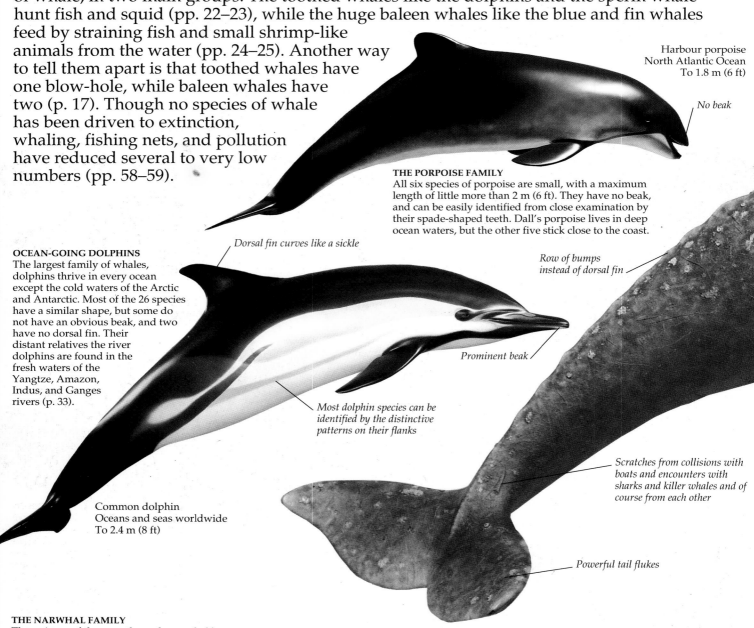

Whales big and small

BOTTLENOSE DOLPHIN
Star of the TV show *Flipper* (p. 54), this is the whale most people know best.

Whales are found in every ocean, from the tropics to the icy waters of the Poles, and in five of the world's greatest rivers. At a maximum length of 31 m (109 ft) and weight of 200 tonnes, the blue whale is the largest animal that has ever lived. At the other end of the scale, the smallest dolphins and porpoises are less than 2 m (6 ft) long, the size of an adult person. There are about 78 species of whale, in two main groups. The toothed whales like the dolphins and the sperm whale hunt fish and squid (pp. 22–23), while the huge baleen whales like the blue and fin whales feed by straining fish and small shrimp-like animals from the water (pp. 24–25). Another way to tell them apart is that toothed whales have one blow-hole, while baleen whales have two (p. 17). Though no species of whale has been driven to extinction, whaling, fishing nets, and pollution have reduced several to very low numbers (pp. 58–59).

Harbour porpoise
North Atlantic Ocean
To 1.8 m (6 ft)

No beak

THE PORPOISE FAMILY
All six species of porpoise are small, with a maximum length of little more than 2 m (6 ft). They have no beak, and can be easily identified from close examination by their spade-shaped teeth. Dall's porpoise lives in deep ocean waters, but the other five stick close to the coast.

Dorsal fin curves like a sickle

OCEAN-GOING DOLPHINS
The largest family of whales, dolphins thrive in every ocean except the cold waters of the Arctic and Antarctic. Most of the 26 species have a similar shape, but some do not have an obvious beak, and two have no dorsal fin. Their distant relatives the river dolphins are found in the fresh waters of the Yangtze, Amazon, Indus, and Ganges rivers (p. 33).

Row of bumps instead of dorsal fin

Prominent beak

Most dolphin species can be identified by the distinctive patterns on their flanks

Scratches from collisions with boats and encounters with sharks and killer whales and of course from each other

Common dolphin
Oceans and seas worldwide
To 2.4 m (8 ft)

Powerful tail flukes

THE NARWHAL FAMILY
The unicorn of the seas, the male narwhal has one of the most remarkable teeth of any animal (pp. 36–37). Like its close relative the beluga, it lives in the icy waters of the Arctic. The third member of this family, the Irrawaddy dolphin, is found far away in tropical Asia. Unlike most other whales, all three species have unfused neck vertebrae, which allow them to turn their heads.

Narwhal
Arctic seas
To 4.7 m (15 ft 5 in)

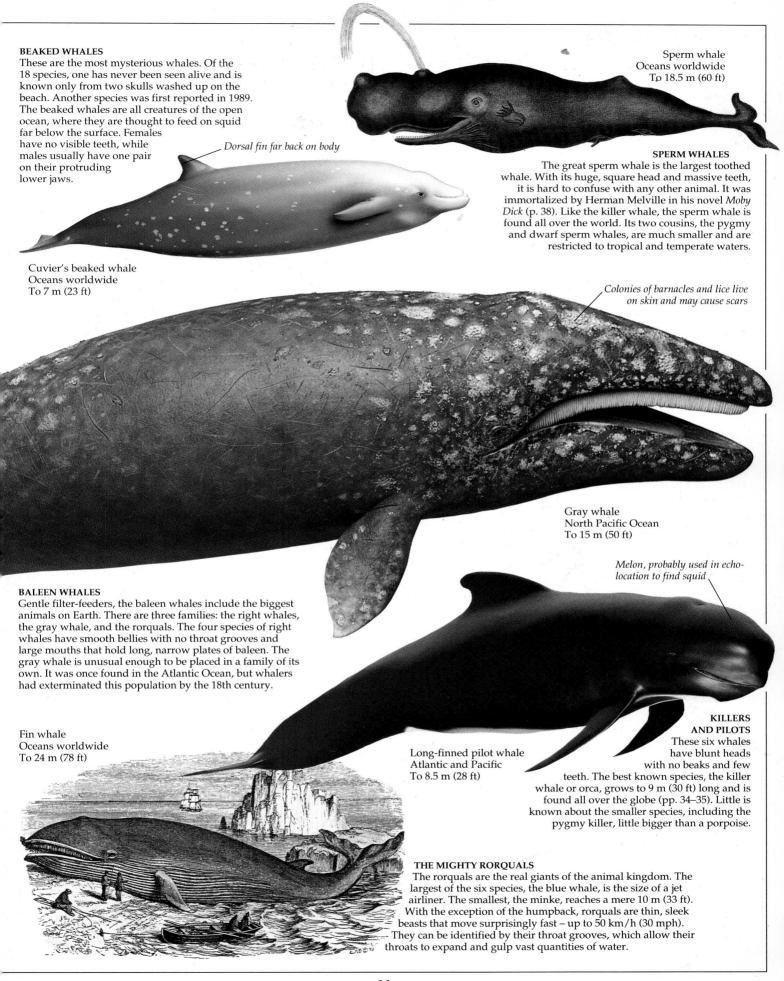

BEAKED WHALES
These are the most mysterious whales. Of the 18 species, one has never been seen alive and is known only from two skulls washed up on the beach. Another species was first reported in 1989. The beaked whales are all creatures of the open ocean, where they are thought to feed on squid far below the surface. Females have no visible teeth, while males usually have one pair on their protruding lower jaws.

Dorsal fin far back on body

Sperm whale
Oceans worldwide
To 18.5 m (60 ft)

SPERM WHALES
The great sperm whale is the largest toothed whale. With its huge, square head and massive teeth, it is hard to confuse with any other animal. It was immortalized by Herman Melville in his novel *Moby Dick* (p. 38). Like the killer whale, the sperm whale is found all over the world. Its two cousins, the pygmy and dwarf sperm whales, are much smaller and are restricted to tropical and temperate waters.

Cuvier's beaked whale
Oceans worldwide
To 7 m (23 ft)

Colonies of barnacles and lice live on skin and may cause scars

Gray whale
North Pacific Ocean
To 15 m (50 ft)

Melon, probably used in echo-location to find squid

BALEEN WHALES
Gentle filter-feeders, the baleen whales include the biggest animals on Earth. There are three families: the right whales, the gray whale, and the rorquals. The four species of right whales have smooth bellies with no throat grooves and large mouths that hold long, narrow plates of baleen. The gray whale is unusual enough to be placed in a family of its own. It was once found in the Atlantic Ocean, but whalers had exterminated this population by the 18th century.

Fin whale
Oceans worldwide
To 24 m (78 ft)

Long-finned pilot whale
Atlantic and Pacific
To 8.5 m (28 ft)

KILLERS AND PILOTS
These six whales have blunt heads with no beaks and few teeth. The best known species, the killer whale or orca, grows to 9 m (30 ft) long and is found all over the globe (pp. 34–35). Little is known about the smaller species, including the pygmy killer, little bigger than a porpoise.

THE MIGHTY RORQUALS
The rorquals are the real giants of the animal kingdom. The largest of the six species, the blue whale, is the size of a jet airliner. The smallest, the minke, reaches a mere 10 m (33 ft). With the exception of the humpback, rorquals are thin, sleek beasts that move surprisingly fast – up to 50 km/h (30 mph). They can be identified by their throat grooves, which allow their throats to expand and gulp vast quantities of water.

Inside the whale

L IKE ITS OUTSIDES, a whale's insides are enormous. A blue whale's arteries are as big as drainpipes and its heart is the size of a small car. Its huge tongue weighs 4 tonnes. Whales have all the same internal organs as other mammals, but many have been modified to cope with life in the sea. For example, they have huge kidneys, which they need to get rid of excess salt. Whales have no hind limbs. But many species have a few vestigial (left-over) back leg bones, reminders of their ancestors that walked on land (pp. 8–9). Baleen whale skeletons are easily identified by their vast mouths, which allow the whales to gulp enormous quantities of seawater (pp. 24–25).

BIG MOUTH
The biggest mouth in the animal kingdom belongs to the blue whale. The huge jaw bones are sometimes erected as arches. This one in the old whaling port of Whitby, England, comes from one of the last blue whales ever caught (pp. 20–21).

THREE DAYS INSIDE THE WHALE
The Bible tells the story of Jonah, who found himself on a boat caught in a storm. The frightened crew threw Jonah overboard, and he was swallowed by a whale. After three days, the whale spat him out, still living, onto a beach (p. 55).

Lumbar (back) vertebrae

Tall processes, where powerful swimming muscles join the backbone

Porpoise flipper

Scapula

Humerus

Radius

Ulna

Metacarpals

Wrist bone

Phalanges

Caudal (tail) vertebrae

Sacral (pelvic) vertebrae

Chevrons, V-shaped bones attached to bottom of vertebrae

Scapula (shoulder blade)

SMELLY BONES
In 1830, visitors flocked to the Royal College of London to admire the bones of a huge right whale. Mounting skeletons of this size is a difficult engineering feat. Many of the bones are too heavy for one man to carry, and have to be held in place by strong steel girders. Whale bones contain a lot of oil and are very smelly before they are cleaned.

Humerus (upper arm bone)

A WHALE'S ARM
A person's arm and a porpoise's flipper look very different on the outside. But under the skin are the same bones, adapted over the millennia to their different functions. A human arm is long and thin, designed for climbing or carrying and manipulating objects. The porpoise's flipper, used for steering and braking, is much shorter and stronger.

Human arm

Radius

Ulna

SPONGY BONE
A land mammal's entire weight is held up by its bones, which are hard and strong. But the great weight of a whale is supported by the sea, and its bones have become soft and spongy. This can be clearly seen in Inuit carvings of whale bones, like this sculpture of a seal.

Wrist bones

Metacarpals (Hand bones)

Phalanges (Finger bones)

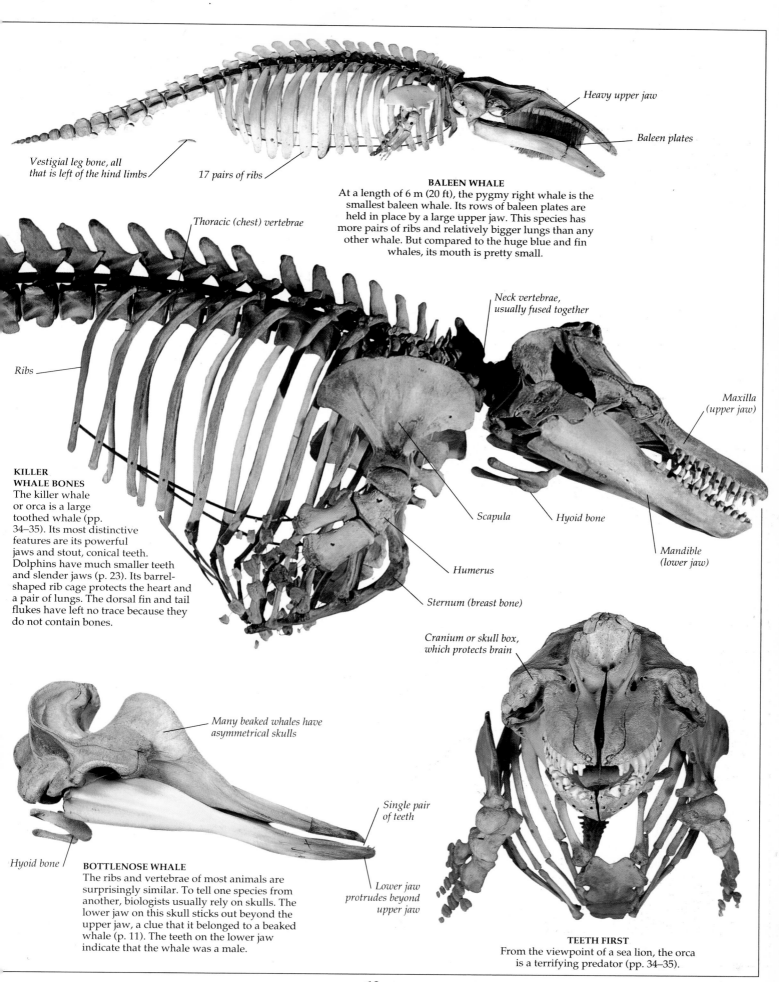

Heavy upper jaw

Baleen plates

Vestigial leg bone, all that is left of the hind limbs

17 pairs of ribs

BALEEN WHALE
At a length of 6 m (20 ft), the pygmy right whale is the smallest baleen whale. Its rows of baleen plates are held in place by a large upper jaw. This species has more pairs of ribs and relatively bigger lungs than any other whale. But compared to the huge blue and fin whales, its mouth is pretty small.

Thoracic (chest) vertebrae

Neck vertebrae, usually fused together

Ribs

Maxilla (upper jaw)

KILLER WHALE BONES
The killer whale or orca is a large toothed whale (pp. 34–35). Its most distinctive features are its powerful jaws and stout, conical teeth. Dolphins have much smaller teeth and slender jaws (p. 23). Its barrel-shaped rib cage protects the heart and a pair of lungs. The dorsal fin and tail flukes have left no trace because they do not contain bones.

Scapula

Hyoid bone

Humerus

Mandible (lower jaw)

Sternum (breast bone)

Cranium or skull box, which protects brain

Many beaked whales have asymmetrical skulls

Single pair of teeth

Hyoid bone

BOTTLENOSE WHALE
The ribs and vertebrae of most animals are surprisingly similar. To tell one species from another, biologists usually rely on skulls. The lower jaw on this skull sticks out beyond the upper jaw, a clue that it belonged to a beaked whale (p. 11). The teeth on the lower jaw indicate that the whale was a male.

Lower jaw protrudes beyond upper jaw

TEETH FIRST
From the viewpoint of a sea lion, the orca is a terrifying predator (pp. 34–35).

13

Seals and sea lions

ALL 34 SPECIES OF SEAL are hunters. Most feed on fish, but some, such as the ferocious leopard seal, eat other seals. There are three families: the true or earless seals (18 species), the eared seals (15 species), and the walrus, which is unusual enough to go in a family of its own. Seals are found all over the world, but they are most common in the icy waters of the Arctic and Antarctic. This is probably because food supplies are more reliable there than in warmer waters. Many species have been reduced to low numbers by human activities. Sealing was just as ruthless as whaling (pp. 52–53), and millions of animals were killed in the last two centuries. Now other seal populations are seriously threatened by pollution (pp. 58-59). Seals spend much of their lives at sea, where they are hard to study. Yet new techniques like satellite tracking (p. 61) are revealing surprising new things about this remarkable and mysterious group of mammals.

ALL IN THE FAMILY
The largest seal, the male elephant seal, grows to 6.5 m (21 ft) and weighs more than four tonnes. The smallest species, the ringed and Baikal seals, still reach 1.37 m (4 ft 6 in) and weigh 64 kg (140 lb).

HAULED OUT
Seals come onto land or ice to give birth. This is called hauling out. Land-breeding seals like the elephant seal gather at a few popular beaches, where competition between bulls (males) can be intense. Bigger, stronger bulls usually triumph, so bulls are usually much bigger than cows (females). Ice-breeding seals like this ringed seal are spread out over a larger area, and bulls and cows are closer to the same size.

TRUE SEALS
This common or harbour seal is a true seal. It has a round, chubby shape and no obvious ear flaps. Like all true seals, it cannot turn its hind flippers under its body, so it cannot climb very well on land. But it moves surprisingly fast on rocky shores. This family includes the world's most common marine mammal, the crabeater seal, and the monk seals, which are among the rarest.

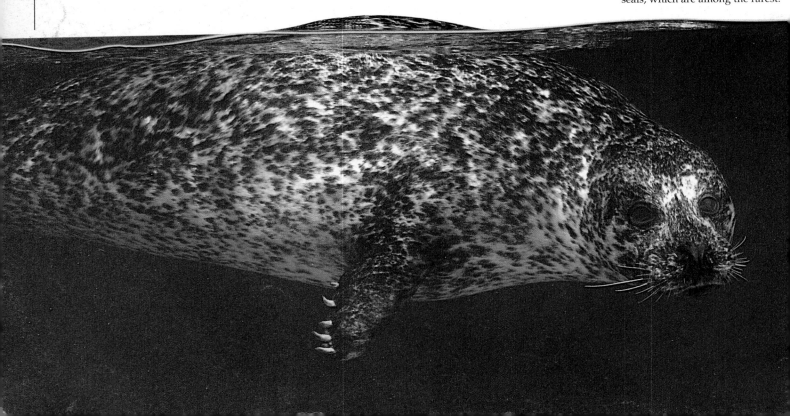

Sensitive whiskers

A COUPLE OF WALRUSES
Walruses live around the moving ice pack of the northern oceans (pp. 42–43). Bulls are about 50 per cent heavier than cows. Both sexes are kept warm by a thick blanket of blubber that can make up half of their body weight. Unlike whales, they are quite hairy, with bushy whiskers to help them find their prey in the dark and murky depths.

COLD COMFORT
In the Arctic, the native Inuit (Eskimo) people have always hunted seals for their meat, fur, and hides (p. 52). They even use seal tendons and bones to make tools or rope. This Inuit stone carving of a seal comes from Frobisher Bay in the Canadian Arctic.

Female or cow walrus

Front flippers steer while swimming

Male or bull walrus

Thick layer of blubber for warmth and protection

Cribbage board carved from a walrus tusk and decorated with seals

WATER HOUNDS
Biologists think seals evolved from dog-like carnivores and share the same ancestors as this jackal. But why did they take to the sea 30 million years ago? Probably because changes in ocean currents created rich new food supplies in the oceans.

EARED SEALS
Like all eared seals, this California sea lion is using its long front flippers to swim through the water; true seals and walruses push with their hind flippers instead (p. 19). There are two main groups of eared seals, the sea lions and the fur seals. They have longer limbs than true seals, and are more agile on land. Like most seals they have large eyes to help them navigate and find prey under water.

Suited to life in the sea

Whales and seals are superbly suited to life in the sea. Because they are supported by the water, they do not need strong legs, and have evolved a sleek shape that slides easily through the water. Many species can swim as fast as a small boat. Powerful muscles in the tail and flanks drive them forwards. Their fins are also streamlined, like a plane's wings. Water is a cold home, and almost all whales and seals have thick layers of blubber which keep them very warm. Many seals also have heavy, oily fur which traps bubbles of air and keeps the animals warm and dry.

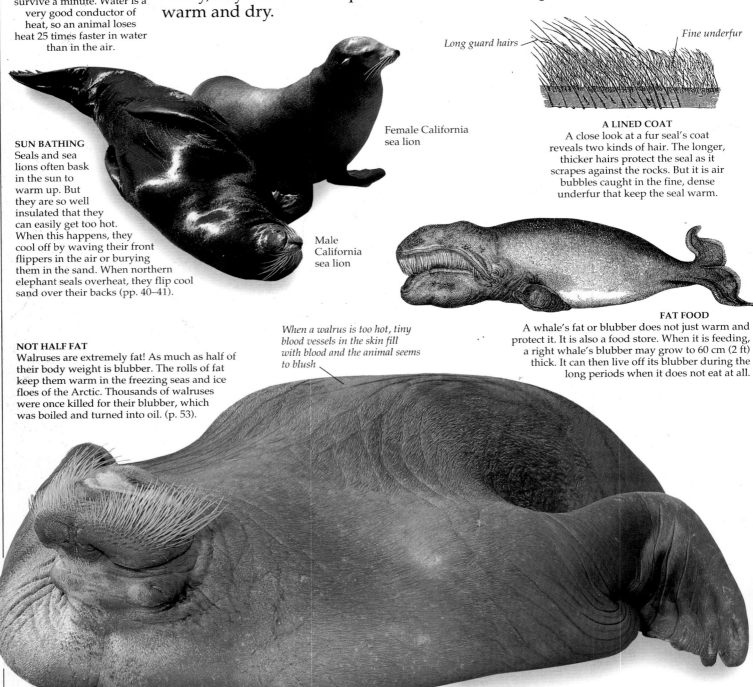

DIVING IN
In most of the world, the ocean is cold enough to take your breath away. In polar seas, a human would barely survive a minute. Water is a very good conductor of heat, so an animal loses heat 25 times faster in water than in the air.

Long guard hairs

Fine underfur

A LINED COAT
A close look at a fur seal's coat reveals two kinds of hair. The longer, thicker hairs protect the seal as it scrapes against the rocks. But it is air bubbles caught in the fine, dense underfur that keep the seal warm.

Female California sea lion

SUN BATHING
Seals and sea lions often bask in the sun to warm up. But they are so well insulated that they can easily get too hot. When this happens, they cool off by waving their front flippers in the air or burying them in the sand. When northern elephant seals overheat, they flip cool sand over their backs (pp. 40–41).

Male California sea lion

FAT FOOD
A whale's fat or blubber does not just warm and protect it. It is also a food store. When it is feeding, a right whale's blubber may grow to 60 cm (2 ft) thick. It can then live off its blubber during the long periods when it does not eat at all.

When a walrus is too hot, tiny blood vessels in the skin fill with blood and the animal seems to blush

NOT HALF FAT
Walruses are extremely fat! As much as half of their body weight is blubber. The rolls of fat keep them warm in the freezing seas and ice floes of the Arctic. Thousands of walruses were once killed for their blubber, which was boiled and turned into oil. (p. 53).

KEEPING YOUR HEAD ABOVE WATER
Humans are poor swimmers. They have no flippers or tail flukes, and get cold because they have hardly any fat. They can barely hold their breath for more than a minute, and have to stick their mouths out of the water to gulp air. Whales have solved all these problems. They have even evolved blow-holes that allow them to breathe through the top of the head.

OPEN...
A whale's blow-hole is a modified nostril that sits on top of its head. Toothed whales like this orca only have one blow-hole. This opens so the whale can snort the old air out of its huge pair of lungs.

... AND CLOSED
Muscles force the blow-hole shut before the orca submerges.

Massive, broad pectoral fin

Coming up to breathe

Taking a breath at sea is a difficult business. Underwater, a whale's blow-hole or a seal's nostrils are shut tight. When the whale surfaces, it breathes out very rapidly. The "blow" forms a fine mist of spray up to 4 m (13 ft) high that can be seen kilometres away. A moment later, the whale breathes in and submerges. Seals breathe out and dive with empty lungs.

DOUBLE-BARRELLED
Baleen whales have two blow-holes that sit side-by-side. Their blow usually looks like a single spray of mist. Only right whales produce distinctive double blows. This minke whale's blow is almost invisible, except in the very coldest Antarctic waters.

Umbilicus (belly button)

Genital slit

Anus

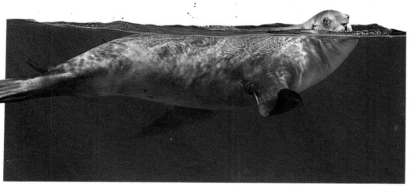

SEAL SOLUTIONS
A seal's eyes and nostrils are at the top of its head, so they stick out of the water while it swims along. Seals and sea lions can even sleep at sea. Some species sleep underwater and somehow manage to wake up every few minutes to breathe. Other kinds of seal sleep at the surface with their nostrils poking out of the water like a snorkel. This is called bottling.

TORPEDO SHAPED
Land animals come in all shapes and sizes. This is because they move in air, which hardly provides any resistance. But swimming through water is hard work, and marine animals all have a similar, stream-lined shape. Even their sexual organs, which would slow them down, are tucked away in a genital slit.

17

Continued on next page

Long pectoral fin or flipper

Throat grooves, a clue that
the humpback is a rorqual

ON A WING AND A SONG
This leaping humpback is showing off its
graceful flippers, much longer than any
other whale's. These are way too long for
simple steering, and are sometimes used to rub
other whales. Humpbacks also slap their flippers
on the water, to make loud splashing noises. This is
called flippering.

TICKET TO RIDE
Barnacles make their homes on the skin of slow-
moving whales such as right and gray
whales. Rorquals like the blue whale
are too fast for most hangers-on.
Sperm whales are slow, but they
regularly shed huge sheets of
dead skin. This makes it hard
for other animals to hitch a
free ride for long

Finding their way around

Whales and seals live in a world that is very different
from our own. Even in the clearest ocean water
visibility is rarely more than 30 m
(100 ft), and they have to hunt at
night or in murky water. Seals
rely on sensitive whiskers.
Toothed whales have
developed a system of echo-
location, using sounds to
find food and their way
around (pp. 26–27). How
whales navigate when they
migrate thousands of
kilometres is another question.
They may have a special magnetic
sense and a built-in compass.

Ear flap

Nose like a dog's

Large eyes

Long whiskers,
specialized hairs used
in close quarters

EYEBALL TO EYEBALL
In the murky ocean, eyes are less use than on
land. This gray whale's eyes are not much
larger than a cow's. They must be pretty
useless while the whale is feeding on the
muddy ocean bottom. But gray whales spy
hop – stick their heads out of the water
to have a look around.

HEAD FULL OF SENSES
For their size, seals have much bigger eyes than whales. Their
senses are similar to a dog's. Apart from the walrus (pp. 42–43),
seals can all see well in and out of the water. This California sea
lion has large eyes and good vision even in dim light.
Its nose is very dog-like. The long whiskers are especially
useful in dark or murky waters.

These muscles contract
to pull tail up

Upstroke begins

Upstroke

Downstroke begins

FISHY TAIL
A fish's tail is vertical, not
horizontal like a whale's. It moves
its tail from side to side to swim.

These muscles
contract to pull tail down

18

Swimming power

Whales are incredible swimmers. Underneath their blubber are huge muscle blocks. The killer whale has been clocked at 56 km/h (34 mph), faster than any other sea mammal. Other species travel thousands of kilometres in their seasonal migrations. The gray whale makes the longest journey, from Mexico to its feeding grounds off Alaska and back again, a round trip of over 20,000 km (12,000 miles).

A whale's tail has many tiny blood vessels and works like a car radiator to cool the animal down

DRIVING FORCE
Like a boat's propeller, a whale's tail drives it through the water. Its flukes – the propeller's blades – are flat and rigid, like tyre rubber. The whale pulls them up and down with large muscles connected to the top and bottom of the spine (p. 12). The whole back third of a killer whale is solid swimming muscle.

Skin covered in a film of oil that helps whale slide through water

Skin feels smooth and rubbery, like a hard-boiled egg

MOSTLY MUSCLE
Do not be fooled by their blubbery appearance. Seals are powerful swimmers, though they cannot compete with whales. Under the fat, this grey seal is mostly muscle.

Open to brake

REAR FLIPPER DRIVE
True seals (p. 14) swim by moving their back flippers and tail from side to side. Young seals sometimes swim by moving both back flippers together. But adult seals usually move them one at a time. True seals of all ages steer with their front flippers.

Closed for cruising

FRONT FLIPPER DRIVE
Like all eared seals (p. 15), fur seals swim with their large front flippers. The rear flippers help to steer. On land, the fur seal can tuck them under the body, so it can clamber around. Like dolphins, some seals "porpoise", leap out of the water when they are swimming fast.

Upstroke begins again

Downstroke ends

THE GREAT SWIMMER
Dolphins are fast and graceful swimmers. People have always admired the apparent ease with which they glide through the water. Dolphins swim by moving their strong tails up and down. Both the upstroke and the downstroke generate power. But dolphins can swim really fast only in short bursts. A close look at a dolphin's skin shows rows of microscopic ridges. How these corrugations help the dolphin is not clear. They may reduce turbulence at high speed.

Downstroke

Front flippers used for steering only

Ocean giants

THE BIGGEST WHALE – and the biggest animal that has ever lived – is the blue whale. Only other baleen whales and the sperm whale come anywhere near its enormous size. The largest living land animal, the bull elephant, could stand on a blue whale's tongue! Even the biggest dinosaur weighed less than a quarter of a large blue whale. Such size has its benefits. Big animals are less likely to be attacked by predators, and it is easier for them to keep warm. The big problem is finding enough food to nourish their awesome bulk.

Pectoral fin

Tail flukes

WHALE LICE
A number of animals make their homes on the great expanse of a whale's skin. Some are harmless hangers-ons, but others, like this whale louse, probably irritate the skin.

TALL TAIL
Unlike some baleen whales, blue whales raise their tails in the air when they dive.

Stubby dorsal fin

A WHALE OF A SHARK
It is no coincidence that whale sharks, the world's largest fish, are also filter feeders. Because animals that feed on plankton do not need to chase individual prey, they do not have to be agile. This has allowed some to grow to great sizes. Whale sharks do not have baleen plates. Instead, they filter food from the water with their gills.

THE WORLD'S BIGGEST BABY
The day it is born, a baby blue whale is already as big as an elephant. It has no baleen plates, and relies entirely on its giant mother's milk. Like seal milk, this is very high in fat. Every day the growing whale drinks about 100 litres (175 pints) of milk and puts on another 90 kg (200 lb). By the time it is weaned, after six or seven months, the young blue whale is already 16 m (54 ft) long.

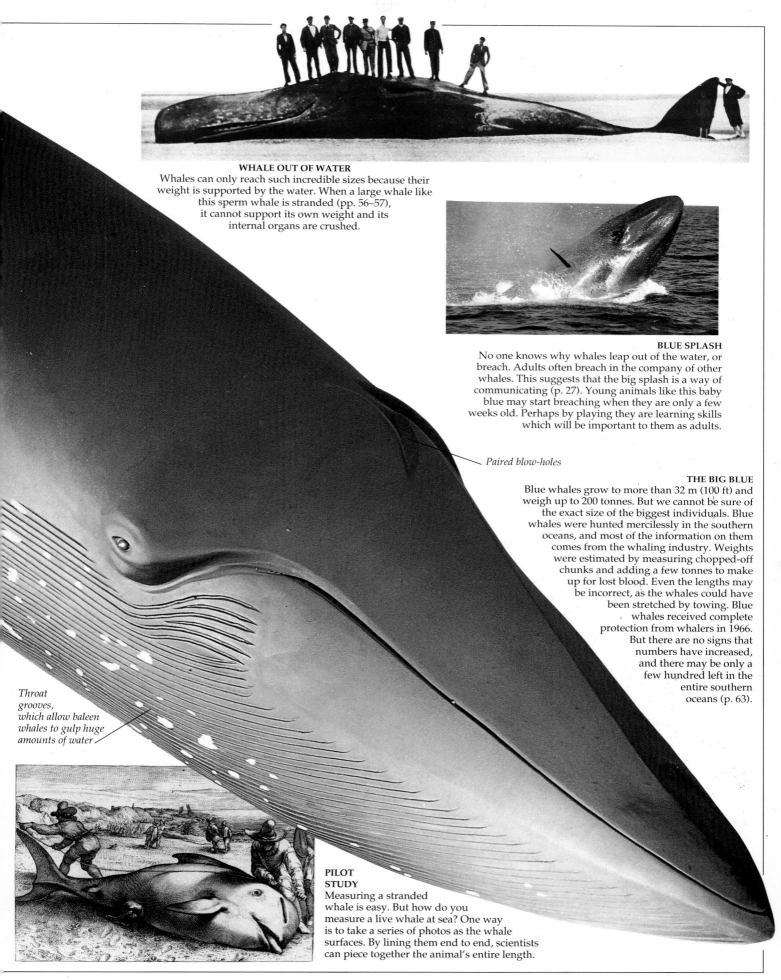

WHALE OUT OF WATER
Whales can only reach such incredible sizes because their weight is supported by the water. When a large whale like this sperm whale is stranded (pp. 56–57), it cannot support its own weight and its internal organs are crushed.

BLUE SPLASH
No one knows why whales leap out of the water, or breach. Adults often breach in the company of other whales. This suggests that the big splash is a way of communicating (p. 27). Young animals like this baby blue may start breaching when they are only a few weeks old. Perhaps by playing they are learning skills which will be important to them as adults.

Paired blow-holes

THE BIG BLUE
Blue whales grow to more than 32 m (100 ft) and weigh up to 200 tonnes. But we cannot be sure of the exact size of the biggest individuals. Blue whales were hunted mercilessly in the southern oceans, and most of the information on them comes from the whaling industry. Weights were estimated by measuring chopped-off chunks and adding a few tonnes to make up for lost blood. Even the lengths may be incorrect, as the whales could have been stretched by towing. Blue whales received complete protection from whalers in 1966. But there are no signs that numbers have increased, and there may be only a few hundred left in the entire southern oceans (p. 63).

Throat grooves, which allow baleen whales to gulp huge amounts of water

PILOT STUDY
Measuring a stranded whale is easy. But how do you measure a live whale at sea? One way is to take a series of photos as the whale surfaces. By lining them end to end, scientists can piece together the animal's entire length.

Teeth for grasping...

MOST WHALES AND SEALS are hunters that catch their slippery prey with rows of sharp teeth. Like most meat-eating mammals (including people), seals and sea lions have a range of different teeth. They grasp their food with powerful canines and incisors and then chew it up with premolars and molars. But toothed whales have simple, peg-like teeth that are all the same shape. Teeth are also used for fighting. One of the most amazing teeth of all, the male narwhal's tusk, is probably used to establish dominance over other males (pp. 36–37). Some beaked whales have teeth that are so strangely shaped that it is hard to imagine what they are for (p. 13)! Perhaps the simple sight of the male's huge teeth makes him irresistible to female whales.

MYSTERY TOOTH
Only mature male sperm whales have teeth. These are huge, up to 25 cm (10 in) long. How females and young males manage to feed and what males use their teeth for are both mysteries.

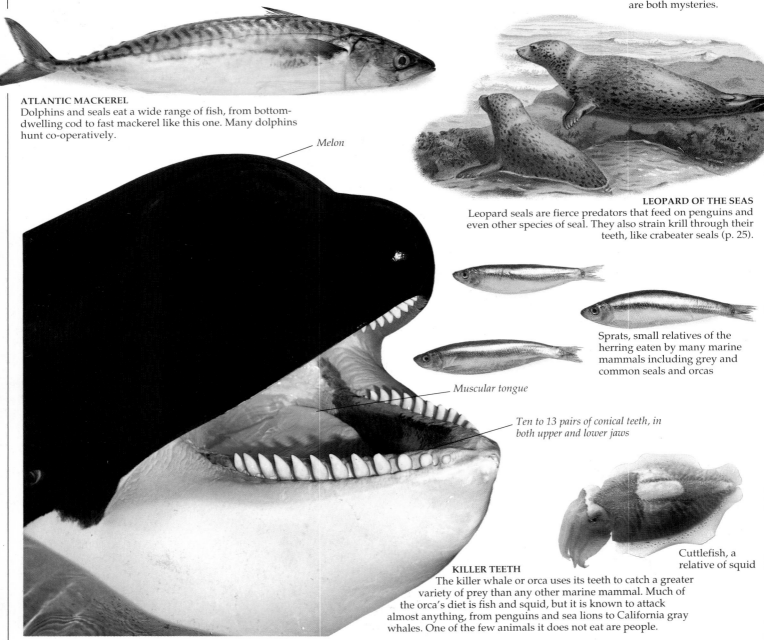

ATLANTIC MACKEREL
Dolphins and seals eat a wide range of fish, from bottom-dwelling cod to fast mackerel like this one. Many dolphins hunt co-operatively.

Melon

LEOPARD OF THE SEAS
Leopard seals are fierce predators that feed on penguins and even other species of seal. They also strain krill through their teeth, like crabeater seals (p. 25).

Sprats, small relatives of the herring eaten by many marine mammals including grey and common seals and orcas

Muscular tongue

Ten to 13 pairs of conical teeth, in both upper and lower jaws

Cuttlefish, a relative of squid

KILLER TEETH
The killer whale or orca uses its teeth to catch a greater variety of prey than any other marine mammal. Much of the orca's diet is fish and squid, but it is known to attack almost anything, from penguins and sea lions to California gray whales. One of the few animals it does not eat are people.

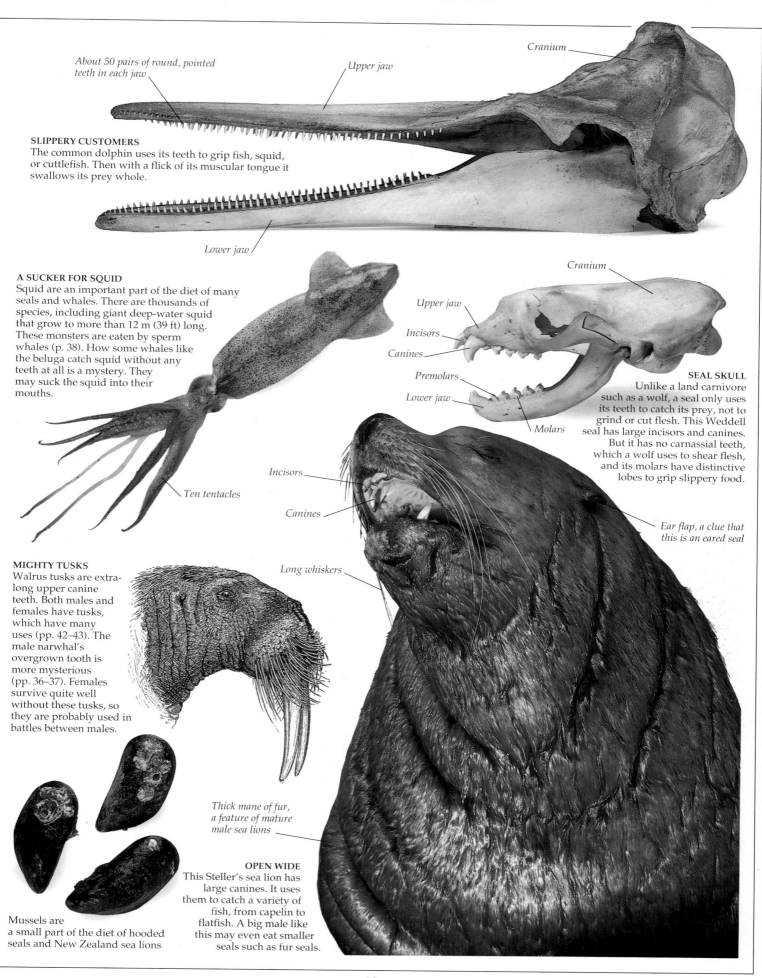

About 50 pairs of round, pointed teeth in each jaw

Upper jaw

Cranium

SLIPPERY CUSTOMERS
The common dolphin uses its teeth to grip fish, squid, or cuttlefish. Then with a flick of its muscular tongue it swallows its prey whole.

Lower jaw

A SUCKER FOR SQUID
Squid are an important part of the diet of many seals and whales. There are thousands of species, including giant deep-water squid that grow to more than 12 m (39 ft) long. These monsters are eaten by sperm whales (p. 38). How some whales like the beluga catch squid without any teeth at all is a mystery. They may suck the squid into their mouths.

Ten tentacles

Cranium

Upper jaw

Incisors

Canines

Premolars

Lower jaw

Molars

SEAL SKULL
Unlike a land carnivore such as a wolf, a seal only uses its teeth to catch its prey, not to grind or cut flesh. This Weddell seal has large incisors and canines. But it has no carnassial teeth, which a wolf uses to shear flesh, and its molars have distinctive lobes to grip slippery food.

Incisors

Canines

Long whiskers

Ear flap, a clue that this is an eared seal

MIGHTY TUSKS
Walrus tusks are extra-long upper canine teeth. Both males and females have tusks, which have many uses (pp. 42–43). The male narwhal's overgrown tooth is more mysterious (pp. 36–37). Females survive quite well without these tusks, so they are probably used in battles between males.

Thick mane of fur, a feature of mature male sea lions

Mussels are a small part of the diet of hooded seals and New Zealand sea lions

OPEN WIDE
This Steller's sea lion has large canines. It uses them to catch a variety of fish, from capelin to flatfish. A big male like this may even eat smaller seals such as fur seals.

... and baleen for filtering

SOME OF THE BIGGEST WHALES feed by filtering. Their filters are baleen plates, huge fringed brushes that hang inside their mouths like giant sieves. The three families of baleen whales have evolved different filtering techniques. But they all draw seawater into their mouths and spit it back out through the baleen, trapping any tasty morsels on the inside. Some feed mainly on krill, small shrimp-like animals found in huge numbers in the southern oceans. Others gulp down entire schools of fish. Most baleen whales pack a whole year's feeding into four or five summer months. In this time their weight may increase by 40 per cent. Much of the energy is stored as fat in preparation for the long migrations to winter breeding grounds (p. 19).

ANOTHER FILTERER
Like whales, flamingos are filter feeders. They have fringed beaks quite similar to baleen plates which they skim through the mud upside-down.

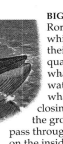

BIG GULP
Rorquals have throat grooves which allow them to expand their mouths to engulf huge quantities of water. A blue whale can take in 60 tonnes of water in one gulp. Then the whale forces the water out by closing its mouth and contracting the grooves. Anything too large to pass through the baleen filter is trapped on the inside and swallowed.

RAISING THE CURTAINS
The right whale's huge head contains 200 to 270 pairs of baleen plates. These hang from the whale's upper jaw like two great curtains with the fringes facing inwards.

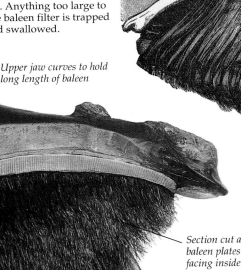

Blow-hole

Upper jaw curves to hold long length of baleen

Section cut away to show baleen plates with fringes facing inside mouth

Massive lower lip

Callosities, areas of rough, horny skin infested with barnacles and lice

The right whale's head can make up a quarter of its body length

SKIMMERS AND GROVELLERS
Right whales usually feed by swimming slowly along with lips parted. Water flows in the front and out the sides of the mouth. Unlike rorquals, they do not open their mouth very wide, but their high, curved lips can hold much longer baleen plates. These are protected by huge lower lips, up to 5 m (16 ft) high in large individuals. The gray whale, the other kind of baleen whale, swims along the bottom making troughs in the mud like a bulldozer. Bowhead whales, a kind of right whale, have been seen feeding in both ways.

Hard outer edge

Inner fringe

FIN WHALE BALEEN
Like your hair and fingernails, baleen is made of a substance called keratin. It grows continually, replacing the fringe as it is worn away.

Top attaches to whale's upper jaw

FITTING TOGETHER
Baleen plates grow from ridges like the ones you can feel on the roof of your mouth. They fit together like cards in a deck.

FINE FILTER
A right whale's baleen grows to 4.3 m (14 ft), much longer than any other whale's. The extremely fine hairs can trap very small animals.

Baleen plate decorated by 19th-century whaler

KRILL
Krill are shrimp-like creatures no longer than your finger. In the summer they occur in enormous swarms that can cover kilometres of the southern oceans, where they are the main food for most baleen whales.

Incisors

Canines

Cheek teeth with three lobes trap krill in mouth

SIEVING SEAL
Despite its name, the crabeater seal does not eat crabs! Instead it uses its strangely shaped teeth to filter krill from the water. This unusual tactic must be successful, because there are more crabeater seals in the world than any other species of seal.

Fine fringe where prey is trapped

Upper jaw of first whale

Upper jaw of second whale

Baleen plate

BLOWING BUBBLES
In some parts of the world, humpback whales use bubbles to herd fish together. This is known as bubble netting. The whale swims in a spiral under the fish, blowing bubbles all the time. Then with its mouth wide open it surfaces in the middle and gulps down the whole school. Humpbacks feed alone or in groups of up to 25 animals. These two are fishing together in the cold waters of the Antarctic.

Lower jaw of first whale, bulging with water and fish

Clicks, barks, and songs

SOUND TRAVELS WELL in water, and the seas are noisy places. Whales and seals live in a world dominated by sound. Dolphins co-ordinate their hunts with whistles and clicks, and male humpbacks sing to attract females. Most large whales make sounds by slapping the surface or breaching – leaping out of the water and coming down with a splash. These splashes can be heard for kilometres and are probably a kind of communication. The most sophisticated use of sound is in echo-location. Only toothed whales and bats have perfected this skill. By sending out a pulse of sound and listening to the returning echo, whales can find their way around and locate fish and squid in the dark water. The biggest toothed whale, the sperm whale, may even stun squid with loud clicks (pp. 38–39). Baleen whales also make loud sounds. Early sailors were terrified when they heard strange rumbles and groans through the hulls of their wooden ships. Like a lot of things whales do, we are just beginning to understand these low-frequency calls, which may travel hundreds of kilometres through the seas.

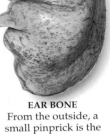

EAR BONE
From the outside, a small pinprick is the only sign of a whale's ear. This dense bone is part of a baleen whale's inner ear.

SIGNATURE WHISTLE
Every dolphin makes its own, unique whistle. Scientists listen to these "signature whistles" to identify individuals. Mothers and their calves have similar-sounding whistles.

WHISTLING WALRUS
Seals that mate in the water make elaborate underwater sounds. Among the noisiest of all are male walruses courting females. Their songs include loud gongs, like underwater bells. They also rise out of the water to bark, whistle, growl, and clack their teeth.

HUMPBACK HITS
Humpback whales are the only non-humans to get into the music charts. Many people enjoy listening to the soothing sounds of humpbacks, belugas, and killer whales. A recording of humpback songs was put aboard the *Voyager* space probe as a greeting from Planet Earth.

LOVE SONG
The male humpback whale sings a beautiful, haunting song for hours on end. All alone, he sings floating motionless in the water with his head hanging down. Like a lot of male birds, humpbacks sing to attract females. The song consists of a number of phrases repeated over and over again. Each individual sings his own song, slightly different from any other, which evolves slowly from year to year. Whales from different areas sing distinctive themes, so scientists can tell which population a whale comes from by its song.

BARKING SEA LION
Seals and sea lions bark a lot. A bark can have many meanings. Male California sea lions bark to frighten off other males. If a female elephant seal (pp. 40–41) is about to be mated by a small male, she will bark to attract the attention of the dominant male, who rushes over and chases the small male away. Seal mothers and pups bark to find each other on the crowded beach (p. 31).

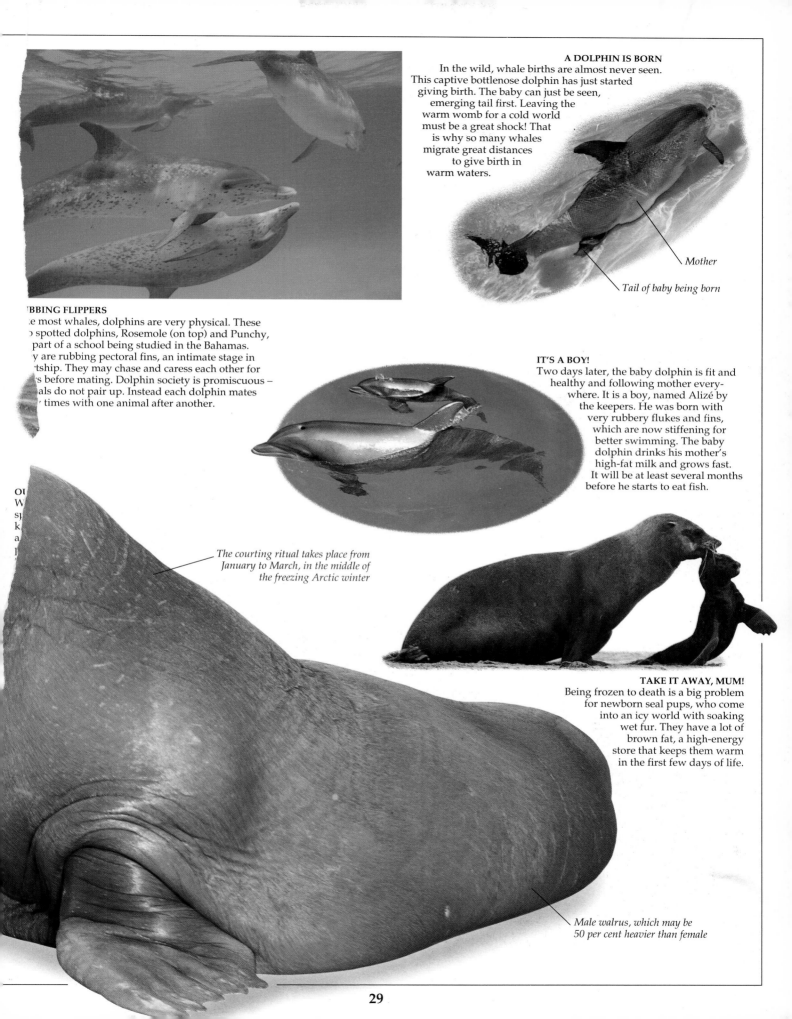

A DOLPHIN IS BORN
In the wild, whale births are almost never seen. This captive bottlenose dolphin has just started giving birth. The baby can just be seen, emerging tail first. Leaving the warm womb for a cold world must be a great shock! That is why so many whales migrate great distances to give birth in warm waters.

Mother

Tail of baby being born

BBING FLIPPERS
e most whales, dolphins are very physical. These
spotted dolphins, Rosemole (on top) and Punchy,
part of a school being studied in the Bahamas.
y are rubbing pectoral fins, an intimate stage in
tship. They may chase and caress each other for
s before mating. Dolphin society is promiscuous –
als do not pair up. Instead each dolphin mates
times with one animal after another.

IT'S A BOY!
Two days later, the baby dolphin is fit and healthy and following mother every-where. It is a boy, named Alizé by the keepers. He was born with very rubbery flukes and fins, which are now stiffening for better swimming. The baby dolphin drinks his mother's high-fat milk and grows fast. It will be at least several months before he starts to eat fish.

OU
W
s
k
a
l

The courting ritual takes place from January to March, in the middle of the freezing Arctic winter

TAKE IT AWAY, MUM!
Being frozen to death is a big problem for newborn seal pups, who come into an icy world with soaking wet fur. They have a lot of brown fat, a high-energy store that keeps them warm in the first few days of life.

Male walrus, which may be 50 per cent heavier than female

Social life

THE SOCIAL LIVES of marine mammals are as varied as the animals themselves. Many seals spend the mating season crowded together on beaches (pp. 28–29). Some whales live alone; others like killer whales spend their whole lives in a small group of close relatives (pp. 34–35). Living in a group protects against attack and allows animals to share in the care of young. Many species of whale also hunt in groups, co-operating to round up fish or even attack other whales or seals (pp. 34–35). Planning and executing complex behaviour like this takes intelligence, and whales seem to be extremely clever. Whales and dolphins are playful and learn new tasks quickly. But does this make them intelligent? It is hard to judge, because our world is so different from theirs.

FIGHTING FOR A SPOT
Good spots for seals and sea lions to come ashore are few and far between. They prefer remote islands and sandbanks, far away from predators such as wolves, bears, or people. So beaches are crowded with aggressive males and females nursing young pups.

SWIMMING LESSONS
Like many young whales, this humpback calf swims close to mother and is pulled along almost effortlessly in her slipstream. The bond between mother and young is very strong in all mammals. Many whales drink mother's milk for several years. A young whale has a lot to learn. Even taking a breath takes some practice, and newborn whales often bob right out of the water. But with a little help from mother, they soon learn to surface gracefully.

FATHER AND SON?
This Steller's sea lion pup is resting on the back of a huge male, who may be its father. Neither the pup nor the male can know for sure. Because of this uncertainty, male seals have little to do with family life beyond mating with females.

SUCKLING SEA LION
This female Steller's sea lion is many times smaller than the male below. She is suckling a young pup. The breeding beaches are so crowded that pups are often crushed when the huge males rush over to mate with females. A female leaves her pup regularly to go fishing. So how does she tell her pup from the hundreds of others on the beach when she gets back? She starts by making a warbling call which attracts any pups nearby. Then she smells and touches any likely-looking youngsters until she is sure she has found hers.

DANCE OF THE DOLPHINS
Dolphin societies are complex and difficult for people to observe. The warm, shallow waters of the Bahamas are one of the few places in the world where schools can be studied over long periods. These spotted dolphins live in schools of fifty or more. Like other social animals, dolphins have disagreements and conflicts. They often confront each other head to head, squawking with open mouths. These conflicts rarely end in physical injury.

Female sperm whale rolling upside-down

Calf

Female sperm whale

Female rolling upside-down

THE DAILY STRUGGLE
These Steller's sea lions are fighting over a fish. During the day, groups of about fifty sea lions have been seen heading out to sea. They work together to find and herd schools of fish or squid. At night, the sea lions usually hunt alone.

COMMUNAL BABYSITTING
Because whales live so long, studying their family lives takes decades. Such studies have only just begun, and little is known about most species. We know that female sperm whales live together in big groups with their young calves (p. 39). Males only spend a few hours with each family group every year. One of the females in this group is probably the mother of the small calf. The other females may be sisters or aunts. When the mother dives deep under water to feed, another female will babysit the calf, protecting it from sharks or killer whales.

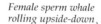

Dolphins and porpoises

PEOPLE HAVE LONG been fascinated by the graceful dolphin. Imagine the magical sight of a school of dolphins leaping for the sheer fun of it, or bow riding, cruising effortlessly on the pressure waves of a boat. The ocean-going dolphins and their close relatives the porpoises are common in all the world's oceans (except for the coldest polar seas). There is still discussion about how the 60 or more species are related. Some species number in the millions and are found all over the world. Others are limited to tiny areas, which makes them more vulnerable. A few species have been reduced to very low numbers by human activity (pp. 58–59). So far, no species has become extinct, and there may just be time to save the two most at risk, the Mexican harbour porpoise (vaquita) and the Chinese river dolphin (p. 63).

PORPOISING
Leaping into the air while swimming along is called porpoising. Strangely enough, most porpoises never do it! The one exception is Dall's porpoise.

LE DAUPHIN
The eldest son of the king of France was given the title *Le Dauphin*, French for "The Dolphin". The title was first adopted by the lords of Viennois, France, who had three dolphins on their coat of arms. When his father died, *Le Dauphin* became king. What happened to the last *Dauphin*, the son of Louis XVI, is still a mystery. His father was executed in 1793, during the French Revolution.

Tail flukes with a central nick, like virtually all whales

WITH TIME ON HIS SIDE
Almost nothing is known about the hourglass dolphin, which gets its name from the pretty black-and-white pattern on its sides. Though they are not shy and often bow ride, they are usually found far out to sea in the remote waters of the southern oceans.

FISHY TAILS
The ancient Minoans and Greeks were fascinated by dolphins, which were much more common in the Mediterranean Sea in their day. Many Greek myths and legends feature dolphins (pp. 54–55). Like most sea-farers, Greek sailors were happy to see dolphins playing near their boats. These animals come from the great palace of Knossos on the island of Crete. They are about 3,500 years old. The fresco painter has given them vertical tails, so they look more like fish than dolphins.

ACROBAT
Dusky dolphins are great leapers. They are coastal animals that live off New Zealand, southern Africa, and South America. Off Peru they are hunted in large numbers for their meat.

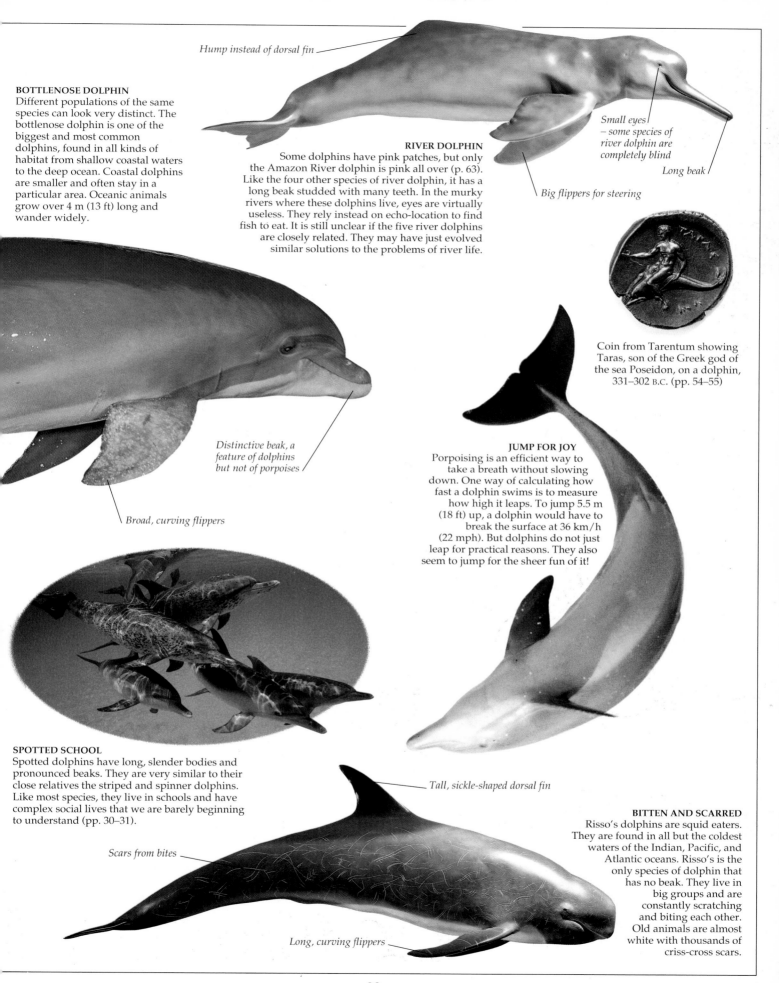

Hump instead of dorsal fin

BOTTLENOSE DOLPHIN
Different populations of the same species can look very distinct. The bottlenose dolphin is one of the biggest and most common dolphins, found in all kinds of habitat from shallow coastal waters to the deep ocean. Coastal dolphins are smaller and often stay in a particular area. Oceanic animals grow over 4 m (13 ft) long and wander widely.

RIVER DOLPHIN
Some dolphins have pink patches, but only the Amazon River dolphin is pink all over (p. 63). Like the four other species of river dolphin, it has a long beak studded with many teeth. In the murky rivers where these dolphins live, eyes are virtually useless. They rely instead on echo-location to find fish to eat. It is still unclear if the five river dolphins are closely related. They may have just evolved similar solutions to the problems of river life.

Small eyes – some species of river dolphin are completely blind

Long beak

Big flippers for steering

Coin from Tarentum showing Taras, son of the Greek god of the sea Poseidon, on a dolphin, 331–302 B.C. (pp. 54–55)

Distinctive beak, a feature of dolphins but not of porpoises

Broad, curving flippers

JUMP FOR JOY
Porpoising is an efficient way to take a breath without slowing down. One way of calculating how fast a dolphin swims is to measure how high it leaps. To jump 5.5 m (18 ft) up, a dolphin would have to break the surface at 36 km/h (22 mph). But dolphins do not just leap for practical reasons. They also seem to jump for the sheer fun of it!

SPOTTED SCHOOL
Spotted dolphins have long, slender bodies and pronounced beaks. They are very similar to their close relatives the striped and spinner dolphins. Like most species, they live in schools and have complex social lives that we are barely beginning to understand (pp. 30–31).

Scars from bites

Tall, sickle-shaped dorsal fin

BITTEN AND SCARRED
Risso's dolphins are squid eaters. They are found in all but the coldest waters of the Indian, Pacific, and Atlantic oceans. Risso's is the only species of dolphin that has no beak. They live in big groups and are constantly scratching and biting each other. Old animals are almost white with thousands of criss-cross scars.

Long, curving flippers

The killer whale

Like the two kinds of pilot whale, this false killer whale is a close relative of the orca. False killers are black all over. They swim with a slow, lazy action. They are the largest whales to bow ride, hitching a free swim from the waves made by boats (p. 32). False killers occasionally eat other marine mammals.

GIANT KILLERS
Imagine the struggle between a great whale and a pod of killers. Even a huge blue whale has no chance against such an attack. Orcas have been seen organizing attacks on all sorts of whales, including a whole pod of sperm whales.

THERE IS NO MISTAKING an orca or killer whale, with its tall dorsal fin, rounded head and startling black-and-white pattern. An adult male can be 9 m (30 ft) long and weigh 10 tonnes. Most of this is muscle, for the orca is the fastest mammal in the seas (p. 19), sprinting at up to 56 km/h (34 mph). This awesome hunter eats almost everything, from small fish to great whales ten times its size. Its ferocious appetite gave it the common name, killer whale. Orcas have no natural predators. Until the 1960s, they were feared and sometimes shot. But opinions have changed, partly because orcas do not seem to eat humans. Orcas are long-lived – a female may reach 90 years old. But they reproduce very slowly, with a calf about every eight years. They live in tight social groups called pods. They hunt co-operatively, and seem to be highly intelligent. Pods of orcas have been seen working together to herd salmon or tip a seal off an ice floe.

Eye

White patch, not eye!

Rounded flippers are black top and bottom

Stiff dorsal fin

White belly

WHY ARE THEY BLACK AND WHITE?
The jet black and shocking white may help to camouflage a killer whale by breaking up its outline. This makes it hard to see as it flits through the water.

SURPRISE!
Orcas are one of the few whales that come onto shore, on purpose (pp. 56–57). On the Peninsula Valdes in Argentina and the Crozet Islands in the Indian Ocean, orcas swim up onto the beach to grab baby sea lions. Then they use their front flippers to turn around and wiggle back into the surf, the sea lion held firmly in their jaws.

LIKE A CAT WITH A MOUSE
All is not yet over for the sea lion. The orca plays with the limp animal like a cat with a mouse. It will fling its prey high into the air with a quick flick of the tail. Young orcas have to learn how to do this, and often join their parents in the game. Finally the terrified sea lion is eaten.

PEA IN A POD
This female killer
is only seven years old and already weighs two tonnes.
Both males and females remain in the same pod as their
mother for life. An older female seems to be in charge of
the pod. Orcas never mate within a pod, but only when
two pods meet. They breach and lobtail a lot during
these exciting encounters.

IT'S A FAMILY AFFAIR
This orca pod lives in British Columbia, Canada. They belong to
the best studied population of whales anywhere in the world.
The 200 plus individuals are easily recognized by the nicks in
their dorsal fins (p. 60) and the shapes of their "saddles", the
grey patches behind the fins. The mature male in this pod has a
huge dorsal fin. These can grow to be 2 m (6 ft) tall.

Melon

SHOULD I STAY OR SHOULD I GO?
Orcas live in every ocean of the world. Researchers in
British Columbia have found two types. Resident
orcas stay in one area, where they eat fish
and squid and make a lot of underwater
sounds. In contrast, transients
(wanderers) roam widely. They
move stealthily and silently
and tackle larger prey
like seals and other
whales.

Blow-hole

BIG SUCKERS
Fishermen and orcas are often in
conflict. In many areas, the fishermen feel that orcas eat valuable
salmon and herring. The whales
are clever. In Alaska, orcas follow
fishing boats and gently suck the
fish from the lines as they are
hauled in. All the fishermen
pull up are the fishes' lips.

The amazing narwhal

THE MYTHICAL UNICORN, a white horse with a horn growing out of its forehead, was really a whale – the "unicorn-whale" or narwhal. Narwhal tusks were on sale in Europe long before the real animal was widely known, so it was easy for imaginative traders to claim that the tusks came from unicorns. Even today the narwhal is a mysterious animal. We are still not certain what its strange overgrown tooth is for, though there are many ideas. Like its close relative the beluga, the narwhal lives in the remote, icy waters of the Arctic, where it is hard to study. Both narwhals and belugas migrate with the seasons, following the receding ice north in the summer and south in the winter. As the sea freezes over, they are sometimes trapped in the ice. They can usually keep breathing holes open, but many narwhals and belugas probably drown when the ice catches them far from open water.

THE UNICORN
In the Middle Ages, narwhal tusks were sold as unicorn horns, which were thought to have magical properties. Cups made from them were supposed to neutralize any poison. The tusks were also ground into a medicinal powder. This was still on sale in Japan in the 1950s under the name of *ikkaku*.

Row of low bumps instead of dorsal fin

Fan-shaped tail, more marked in older narwhals

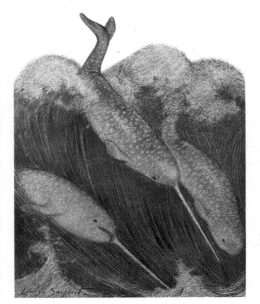

WHAT'S IT FOR?
People have suggested all kinds of uses for the narwhal's tusk. Some guess that the giant tooth is used to spear fish or to break holes in the ice. Others say the narwhal may use it as a hoe to root out animals on the ocean floor. But all these ideas are probably wrong, because they do not explain why males have tusks, while females survive very well without them!

Right tooth, which usually does not grow beyond the gums

Pectoral flipper

Left tooth or tusk grows in an anti-clockwise spiral

LONG IN THE TOOTH
A bottom view of a male narwhal's skull shows the roots of its mighty tooth. All narwhals have two teeth, though in females they almost never grow beyond the gums. The same is usually true for a male's right tooth, while the left grows out to become the tusk. In adults, the tusk can be 3 m (10 ft), more than half as long as the whale's body. Every now and then a female grows a tusk, or a male grows two. Two-tusked skulls were especially prized, and there are quite a few of them in museums.

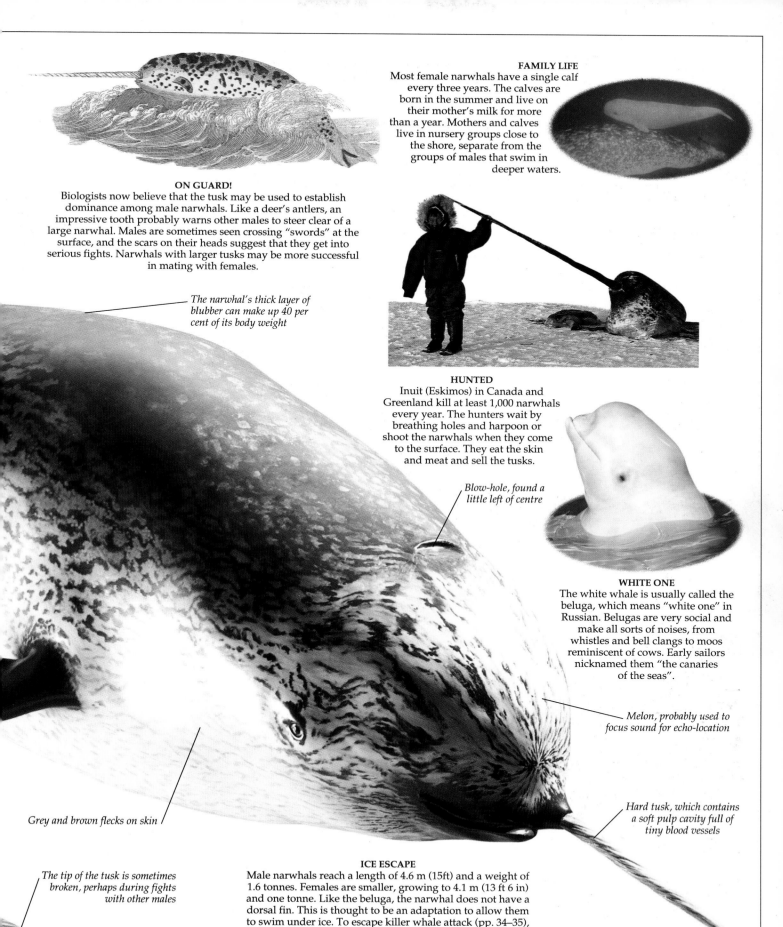

ON GUARD!

Biologists now believe that the tusk may be used to establish dominance among male narwhals. Like a deer's antlers, an impressive tooth probably warns other males to steer clear of a large narwhal. Males are sometimes seen crossing "swords" at the surface, and the scars on their heads suggest that they get into serious fights. Narwhals with larger tusks may be more successful in mating with females.

The narwhal's thick layer of blubber can make up 40 per cent of its body weight

FAMILY LIFE

Most female narwhals have a single calf every three years. The calves are born in the summer and live on their mother's milk for more than a year. Mothers and calves live in nursery groups close to the shore, separate from the groups of males that swim in deeper waters.

HUNTED

Inuit (Eskimos) in Canada and Greenland kill at least 1,000 narwhals every year. The hunters wait by breathing holes and harpoon or shoot the narwhals when they come to the surface. They eat the skin and meat and sell the tusks.

Blow-hole, found a little left of centre

WHITE ONE

The white whale is usually called the beluga, which means "white one" in Russian. Belugas are very social and make all sorts of noises, from whistles and bell clangs to moos reminiscent of cows. Early sailors nicknamed them "the canaries of the seas".

Melon, probably used to focus sound for echo-location

Grey and brown flecks on skin

Hard tusk, which contains a soft pulp cavity full of tiny blood vessels

The tip of the tusk is sometimes broken, perhaps during fights with other males

ICE ESCAPE

Male narwhals reach a length of 4.6 m (15ft) and a weight of 1.6 tonnes. Females are smaller, growing to 4.1 m (13 ft 6 in) and one tonne. Like the beluga, the narwhal does not have a dorsal fin. This is thought to be an adaptation to allow them to swim under ice. To escape killer whale attack (pp. 34–35), narwhals often stay close to the pack ice. The killer whales leave them alone for fear of hitting their sensitive dorsal fins on the ice.

The sperm whale

SPERM WHALES HAVE THE LARGEST brains that have ever existed and a family life that spans the globe. They are creatures of the open ocean that dive to incredible depths to feed on squid, a food resource that is out of reach of most other predators. A male sperm whale eats more than a tonne of squid a day, and every year sperm whales eat more food than the total amount caught by all the world's fishermen. We still know little about how the whale hunts in its dark underwater world. The function of its huge square forehead is also unclear. It may help the sperm whale dive to such amazing depths. The whale may even use its head to produce powerful clicks to stun its prey.

THE WHITE WHALE
The most famous sperm whale is Moby Dick, the hero of Herman Melville's novel. It is the story of Captain Ahab, who has lost a leg in a battle with the huge white whale. He becomes obsessed with killing the whale and hunts it all over the globe. In the end, Moby Dick sinks the ship and the captain goes down with it. Albino (white) sperm whales do occur, but they are very rare.

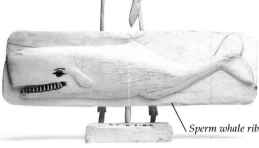

Sperm whale rib

MADEIRA SPERM WHALE
Catching sperm whales from open boats was a dangerous occupation (pp. 46–47). Until a few years ago, whales were still killed in this way off Madeira and the Azores Islands in the Atlantic Ocean. The Azores population is still healthy, but there are few sperm whales left off Madeira.

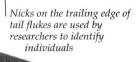

Nicks on the trailing edge of tail flukes are used by researchers to identify individuals

PYGMY SPERM
Almost nothing is known about the pygmy and dwarf sperm whales, the other members of the family. Both are relatively small, less than 3 m (10 ft) long. Like the sperm whale, they are deep divers that live in the open ocean.

FOUL-SMELLING PEARL
Once worth its weight in gold, ambergris is a foul-smelling wax that was used to make perfumes. It is occasionally secreted in the sperm whale's guts, perhaps around squid beaks. For whalers, finding a lump of ambergris was a valuable prize. It sometimes washes ashore in places like the Maldive Islands, to the delight of the local people.

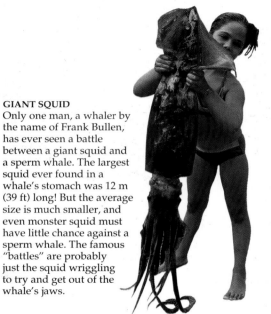

GIANT SQUID
Only one man, a whaler by the name of Frank Bullen, has ever seen a battle between a giant squid and a sperm whale. The largest squid ever found in a whale's stomach was 12 m (39 ft) long! But the average size is much smaller, and even monster squid must have little chance against a sperm whale. The famous "battles" are probably just the squid wriggling to try and get out of the whale's jaws.

MAKING A SPLASH
This sperm whale is lobtailing – lifting its muscular tail flukes into the air and slamming them down on the water. Like breaching (p. 27), this is probably a way of communicating. It is usually females that lobtail, often in the presence of males. The big splashes made by lobtailing and breaching can be heard under water a long way off.

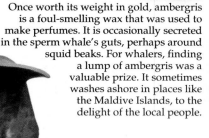

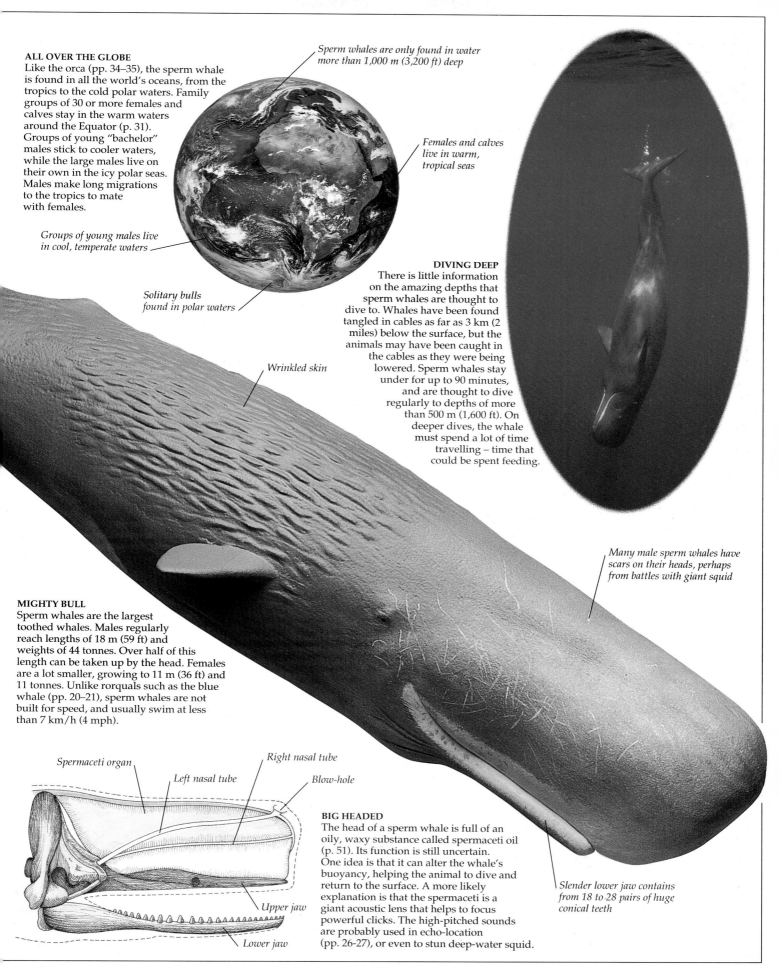

ALL OVER THE GLOBE
Like the orca (pp. 34–35), the sperm whale is found in all the world's oceans, from the tropics to the cold polar waters. Family groups of 30 or more females and calves stay in the warm waters around the Equator (p. 31). Groups of young "bachelor" males stick to cooler waters, while the large males live on their own in the icy polar seas. Males make long migrations to the tropics to mate with females.

Sperm whales are only found in water more than 1,000 m (3,200 ft) deep

Females and calves live in warm, tropical seas

Groups of young males live in cool, temperate waters

Solitary bulls found in polar waters

Wrinkled skin

DIVING DEEP
There is little information on the amazing depths that sperm whales are thought to dive to. Whales have been found tangled in cables as far as 3 km (2 miles) below the surface, but the animals may have been caught in the cables as they were being lowered. Sperm whales stay under for up to 90 minutes, and are thought to dive regularly to depths of more than 500 m (1,600 ft). On deeper dives, the whale must spend a lot of time travelling – time that could be spent feeding.

Many male sperm whales have scars on their heads, perhaps from battles with giant squid

MIGHTY BULL
Sperm whales are the largest toothed whales. Males regularly reach lengths of 18 m (59 ft) and weights of 44 tonnes. Over half of this length can be taken up by the head. Females are a lot smaller, growing to 11 m (36 ft) and 11 tonnes. Unlike rorquals such as the blue whale (pp. 20–21), sperm whales are not built for speed, and usually swim at less than 7 km/h (4 mph).

Spermaceti organ

Left nasal tube

Right nasal tube

Blow-hole

BIG HEADED
The head of a sperm whale is full of an oily, waxy substance called spermaceti oil (p. 51). Its function is still uncertain. One idea is that it can alter the whale's buoyancy, helping the animal to dive and return to the surface. A more likely explanation is that the spermaceti is a giant acoustic lens that helps to focus powerful clicks. The high-pitched sounds are probably used in echo-location (pp. 26-27), or even to stun deep-water squid.

Upper jaw

Lower jaw

Slender lower jaw contains from 18 to 28 pairs of huge conical teeth

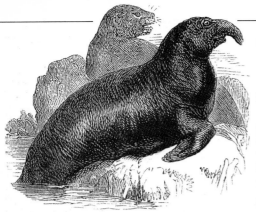

The elephant seal

THE ELEPHANT seal gets its name from the male's huge, swollen nose. He uses it in an incredible mating ritual. Elephant seals are enormous, up to three tonnes. They come ashore in large groups to mate, give birth, and suckle their young. There is constant activity on the crowded beaches as the biggest, strongest males battle for places among the females, while less dominant males hang around the edges. The pups and females grunt and groan and the males roar. These beaches are dangerous places for people, who could be attacked by an aggressive male. There are two species of elephant seal, southern and northern. Though they live thousands of kilometres apart, they are thought to be closely related. Northern elephant seals are found off the west coast of North America, where they haul out (come ashore) on isolated islands from San Francisco to Baja, Mexico. Southern elephant seals are found all around the Antarctic.

NOSE JOB
Most animals just use their noses to smell. But the elephant's trunk is like an arm, good for picking up objects, even spraying water like a hose. The sperm whale has the largest nose of all. It probably uses this to focus sounds (p. 38–39).

WHAT A SCHNOZZ!
Male elephants seals are up to ten times heavier than females (which do not have such large noses). Every male tries to control a harem (group) of females and keep other males away. He scares off rivals by bellowing, rearing up on his belly, and filling his nose with air. Hopefully that other males will think he is huge and leave him in peace.

BATTLE OF THE GIANTS
These two males are fighting for control of a beach crowded with females. These battles start with a lot of huffing and puffing and showing off of noses. Usually the smaller male then sneaks away and avoids a fight. But two big males may have a violent showdown. Most large males are covered in scars and bitemarks.

The elephant seal is a true seal, and cannot tuck its hind flippers under its body

BLUBBERING ABOUT
Elephant seals are deep divers. They are known to reach depths of over a kilometre below the surface (p. 61). At such depths the pressure is enormous. A fur coat would not keep the animal warm, because the bubbles trapped between the hairs would be compressed to almost nothing (p. 16). Instead elephant seals stay warm with thick layers of blubber.

Cranium (brain case)

Processes where strong neck muscles attach to spine

Neck vertebrae, not fused like a whale's

Massive lower jaw

Thoracic (chest) vertebrae

Tall processes, where swimming muscles attach to spine

Clavicle (collar bone)

Scapula (shoulder blade)

Humerus

Lumbar (lower back) vertebrae

Fibia

Sternum

Ribs

Pelvic girdle (hips)

Tibia

BARE BONES OF AN ELEPHANT SEAL
A seal's skeleton is more like a dog's than a whale's (pp. 12–13). The legs are modified into strong flippers, with long, strong "finger" bones. On land an elephant seal cannot lift its whole weight with its flippers, but keeps its belly on the ground and moves by flexing its back.

Femur

Phalanges (finger bones)

Wrist bones

Phalanges (toe bones)

TRUE LOVE?
The female elephant
seal (on the left) cannot really say no when
it comes to mating. The huge male pins her
down and may bite her neck to keep her
still. As soon as he finishes, he moves on to
the next female.

MILK LIKE MAYONNAISE
Seal milk looks like mayonnaise.
Southern elephant seal milk contains up
to 43 per cent fat. The mother does not
eat at all for the whole three to four
weeks of suckling. She loses a lot of
weight, while the pup puts it on fast.
Some northern elephant seal pups grow
even faster by sneaking milk from
several females.

*Half of body weight
may be blubber*

*Large front flippers,
used to steer while
swimming*

POLLUTED BEACH
A big threat to elephant seals these days is
pollution. Most of this ugly rubbish is
harmless. But seals often get tangled in
packing straps and nets. As the seal
grows, its neck or flipper is cut by the
hard plastic. This is a slow and painful
way to die.

WE ARE FAMILY
The northern elephant seal was
hunted almost to extinction at the
end of the 19th century (pp. 52–53).
When the killing stopped, there
were less than a hundred seals
left. This small band of survivors
made an incredible recovery,
and all the animals alive today
are descended from them.
The population has reached
120,000. But all these seals
are closely related, and
people are worried that
they may suffer from
inbreeding.

*Hind flippers, the seal's
driving force*

Hunting the mighty whale

PEOPLE HAVE HUNTED WHALES for two thousand years. For early whalers like the Vikings, the whale was a sea monster to be conquered in a desperate battle. In the last century, whaling was a dangerous occupation. Ships set sail for the frozen and uncharted Arctic. When a whale was seen, tiny boats were lowered and rowed silently up to the unsuspecting giant. Hand harpoons were thrown into the whale. In the struggle, boats were often overturned and men drowned. Even in those early days, far too many whales were killed and the whalers had to move from place to place to find new stocks (populations) to hunt. Soon large Yankee (American) ships were sailing the world in search of whales.

YANKEE WHALING BOAT
When the lookout saw a whale spouting, he let out the traditional cry "Thar she blows!" Then boats were lowered and the whale was harpooned. This model of a Yankee whaling boat is made from sperm whale bones. In the Arctic, the whale was towed ashore to be cut up and boiled down for its oil. But sperm whales are creatures of the open ocean (pp. 38–39), and Yankee whalers had to process them aboard ship.

KEEPING A GRIP
Keeping your footing on a whale's slippery back was no easy task. So the whalers who flensed (cut up) the whale wore sharp spurs on their boots, like the crampons used by mountaineers.

A WHALER'S TOOLS
Whalers took a variety of tools on their long voyages. Harpoons were thrown from a distance. They were attached to a coil of rope which played out as the whale dived. When the injured, exhausted whale came up for the last time, it was killed with a lance from close quarters. The dead whale was then cut up with various flensing tools.

WHALE OF A POT
Blubber pots were mounted in pairs on the ship's deck. They were filled with blubber and a fire was lit below to extract the oil. This was ladled off, cooled, and poured into storage casks.

BENT IN BATTLE
Harpoons were made of soft iron, so they could be straightened if they were bent by the whale.

Bowsprit

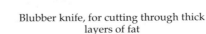

Lance, used to kill whale

Blubber knife, for cutting through thick layers of fat

Dolphin striker, which holds down bowsprit

Flensing spade, for peeling back rolls of blubber

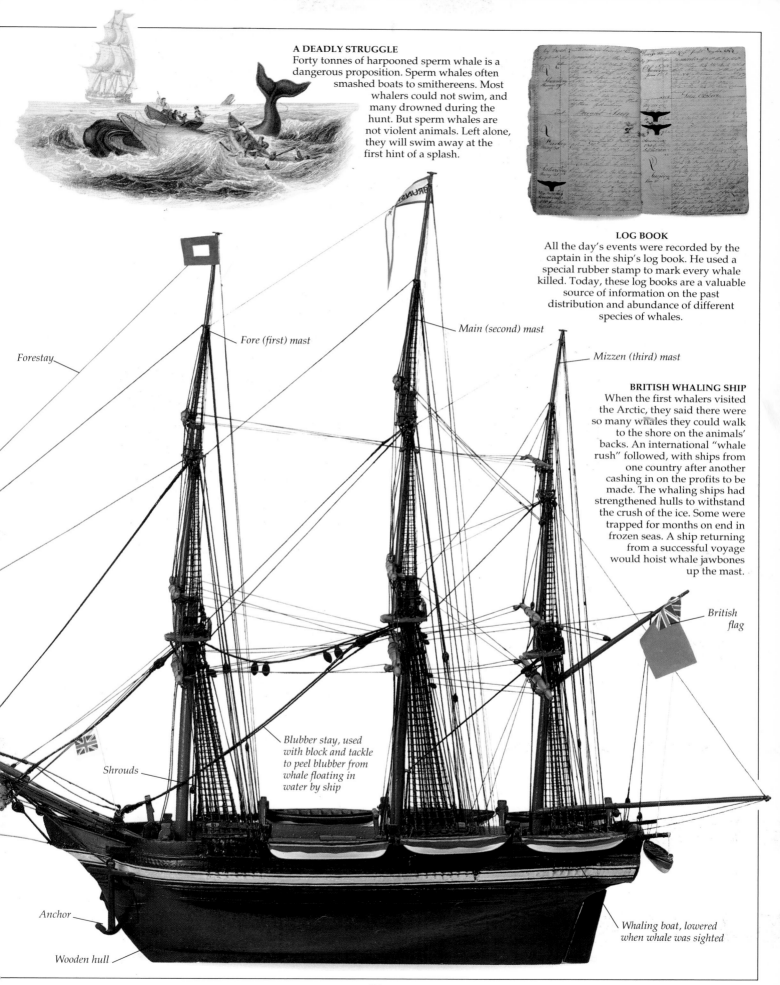

A DEADLY STRUGGLE
Forty tonnes of harpooned sperm whale is a dangerous proposition. Sperm whales often smashed boats to smithereens. Most whalers could not swim, and many drowned during the hunt. But sperm whales are not violent animals. Left alone, they will swim away at the first hint of a splash.

LOG BOOK
All the day's events were recorded by the captain in the ship's log book. He used a special rubber stamp to mark every whale killed. Today, these log books are a valuable source of information on the past distribution and abundance of different species of whales.

BRITISH WHALING SHIP
When the first whalers visited the Arctic, they said there were so many whales they could walk to the shore on the animals' backs. An international "whale rush" followed, with ships from one country after another cashing in on the profits to be made. The whaling ships had strengthened hulls to withstand the crush of the ice. Some were trapped for months on end in frozen seas. A ship returning from a successful voyage would hoist whale jawbones up the mast.

Forestay

Fore (first) mast

Main (second) mast

Mizzen (third) mast

British flag

Blubber stay, used with block and tackle to peel blubber from whale floating in water by ship

Shrouds

Anchor

Wooden hull

Whaling boat, lowered when whale was sighted

Whaling in the 20th century

STEAM-POWERED SHIPS and explosive harpoons revolutionized whaling. With these advances, whalers could hunt the fast rorquals like fin whales and the mighty blue (pp. 20–21). No animal was safe. The whalers travelled the world, slaughtering population after population. By the turn of the century, they had arrived in the remote, inhospitable waters of the Antarctic. At first the whalers towed dead whales back to shore stations on islands like South Georgia. Then factory ships that could process dead whales at sea one after another were built. In 1988, a worldwide moratorium (ban) finally brought a pause in commercial whaling. By then, the whalers were under a lot of pressure from conservationists. But the main reason most countries stopped was economic – there were not enough whales left!

WHAT A FLUKE!
A whaler is dwarfed by a sperm whale's tail fluke. Since 1946, whaling has been regulated by the International Whaling Commission (IWC). This began as a whaler's club that tried to control the price of whale oil. But now the IWC is looking very carefully at ways to protect the future of whales. It banned the commercial whaling of sperm whales after 1984.

HITTING THE WHALE
It is virtually impossible to kill a whale humanely. The vital organs are hard to hit from a moving vessel. Often the harpoons do not explode. Most whales are killed within a few minutes, but some struggle in agony for more than half an hour.

Tip loaded with grenade which explodes inside whale

Barbs open on impact so harpoon is embedded in flesh

FLENSING A BLUE
Before whaling started in the Antarctic, there were about 250,000 blue whales there. Now there may only be a few hundred left. This dead giant was 27.4 m (90 ft) long. The next species to be hunted was the smaller fin whale. Once they became hard to find, the whalers moved on to even smaller sei whales.

HARPOONING DOLPHINS
This whaler is harpooning dolphins that have come to bow ride on his boat (p. 32). Even today, there are few restrictions on the hunting of small whales, which are not covered by the IWC. In many countries, dolphins and porpoises are killed for food, sport, or even crab bait.

48

THE BOWHEAD HUNT
The Inuit have hunted small numbers of bowhead whales for many centuries. But because of European whaling, the bowhead is now on the verge of extinction (p. 63). These Inuit whalers are flensing (cutting up) a dead whale. They still kill a few bowheads every year. This is not considered a commercial hunt, because no part of the whale is sold.

THAR SHE BLEEDS
Until very recently, sperm whales were caught off the Atlantic islands of the Azores and Madeira (p. 38). The whalers used small *canoas* (sailing canoes) and hand harpoons, like the Yankee whalers of last century. They towed the dead whales back to stations on shore to be processed. Every year, the Azoreans managed to catch several hundred sperm whales with these primitive methods.

Calibrated sight

Muzzle

Trigger

MUZZLE-LOADING HARPOON GUN
Norwegian technology and expertise were important in developing the whaling industry all over the world. The Norwegians set up whaling operations in many countries, including Japan. This harpoon gun was made in Norway in 1925. It was used in Antarctic whaling. The gun was mounted on the bow of a boat and loaded with a harpoon with an explosive tip. It was solidly made to absorb the recoil, and accurately balanced so it was easy to aim.

Cradle which holds muzzle and pivots

FACTORY SHIP
This dead minke whale is being dragged into a Japanese factory ship. It will be cut up and processed on board. The countries that want to continue whaling have focused on minke whales, which reach a top length of 10 m (33 ft). In the past, this was too small to bother with. There are still a fair few minkes in the southern oceans, but whaling in the north may have reduced some populations by over half.

Oils, brushes, and corsets

THE EARLY WHALERS SUFFERED incredible hardships so the world could have brushes, oil, soap, candles, umbrellas, and corsets. In an age before petroleum or plastics, whales provided valuable raw materials for thousands of everyday objects. Right whales were killed for their oil and baleen (pp. 24–25). The oil was refined and sold to be burnt in lamps. Baleen, often given the misleading name "whalebone", was a tough, springy material used to stiffen corsets and as bristles for brushes. Sperm whales were hunted for the oil in their heads. At first this was burnt in lamps and used to make candles. As the machine age unfolded, sperm oil became a high-grade lubricant for motors and cars. The whaling of other species ended because there were not enough whales left. But sperm whaling ended with the discovery of petroleum, a cheaper source of oil. Nowadays, alternatives have been found for all whale products. But whale meat has become a gourmet food item in Japan, where it can sell for $160 a kilo.

TIGHT FIT
Women wore very uncomfortable clothes years ago. They were squeezed into elaborate corsets stiffened with baleen ("whalebone").

Necklace made from whale bone

PILLS AND SOAP
Like all oils, whale oil can be turned into soap through a simple chemical process. Early in the 20th century, foods such as margarine and ice cream were also made from whale oil.

SCRAPING A LIVING
Many whale-related industries were set up in whaling ports. Here baleen from right whales is being scraped clean before being manufactured into the various products on these pages. Two whaling ships can be seen in the port in the background.

Chimney sweep's brush with baleen bristles

Floor brush with baleen bristles

Comb made from baleen

BALEEN BRUSHES
These days most brushes are made from plastics. But a hundred years ago, baleen was shredded to make brush bristles.

Hair brush with baleen bristles

SCRIMSHAW

On their long voyages, whalers passed the time decorating whales' teeth and bones. This is called scrimshaw. The designs were made more visible by rubbing soot into the scratches.

BURNING BRIGHT

What a live sperm whale does with the litres of oil in its huge head is still a mystery (pp. 38–39). Whalers had no problems finding a use for the oil. These spermaceti oil candles burn with a bright, clear flame. Engravings of Yankee whalers often show them bathed in the light of a thousand such lamps and candles.

SPERMACETI CANDLES from NANTUCKET ISLAND, MASS.

UMBRELLA

Old umbrellas had ribs made of springy baleen. Nowadays these have been replaced with steel or plastic.

Baleen ribs

GET YOUR WHALE MEAT!

With the advent of plastics and petroleum, the market for whale products almost disappeared. Now the main product is whale meat for eating. This Norwegian fishing boat has caught a whale to supplement its income. Some of the meat is sold locally on the quay, but most is exported to Japan.

ONE PAIR DAWBARN'S BL...
Genuine **WHITE WHALE Boot Laces**
HAND-CUT WALONGA BRAND NO TAGS
MADE IN ENGLAND MARKET HARBOROUGH, LEICESTERSHIRE
These Laces should not be pulled or jerked violently when first placed in the shoes

BELUGA BOOT LACES

These boot laces were made from the skin of belugas (white whales, p. 37). Whale oil was used to soften all kinds of leather.

Dyed baleen bristles ready to be made into brushes

Whale meat extract

Whale meal

Whale liver oil

Sperm oil

RAW MATERIALS

Whale meat extract was used to manufacture margarine. Animal feed and pet food were made from whale meal. Whale liver oil was a source of vitamin A, and sperm oil was a machine lubricant.

Handle made from whale's bone

Seal hunting

MOVING TARGET
The Inuit hunted seals from small sealskin boats called kayaks. The harpoon line was attached to a float, a seal bladder blown up like a balloon. If the harpooned seal put up a struggle, the hunter would throw the line and float overboard rather than risk capsizing the kayak.

LIKE WHALES, seals have been hunted for centuries. The story of sealing is not as well known, but it is just as bloody. The Inuit (Eskimo) people of the Arctic have always hunted seals. They made use of every bit of the seal, eating its meat, making clothes and boats from its skin, and burning seal oil in lamps. They never killed a lot of seals. But in the last two centuries, reckless commercial hunting did great damage to many seal populations. In the southern oceans, millions of elephant and fur seals were killed.

Huge numbers of walruses died in the Arctic, and the northern elephant seal was brought within a whisker of extinction (p. 41). But unlike whales, many seal populations have recovered. Sealing continues today, but the market for seal products is small.

Flint spearhead

Bone harpoon

Shaft carved from a whale penis bone

Inuit stone sculpture of seal hunter, from northern Canada

Head carved from seal bone

Wooden paw

Soapstone

Bone knife

ICE SCRATCHER
Another way of catching seals is to build a small shelter on the ice right next to a breathing hole. The Inuit hunter would stand by the hole for hours on end, a harpoon raised ready to strike. To stop his feet from freezing, he stood on a folded sealskin. The first sign of a seal would be the sound of its breathing. This scratcher from Alaska was rubbed on the ice to attract curious seals to the surface.

Seal breathing hole

Hunter dragging dead seal

Open sea   *Hunter in kayak*

SEALING SCENE
This seal hunting scene was etched onto a walrus tusk (pp. 42–43). The successful hunters are dragging dead seals with harpoon lines. Many Inuit myths are about seals. They believe that seals are always thirsty, so when one is killed, the hunter puts water to its lips.

Harpoon thrower

Figure of hunter

Harpoon lashed to deck

Wooden handle

HARPOON
Wood is scarce in the Arctic. This harpoon is made from driftwood, stone, and whale bones.

MODEL HUNTER
This model of a man in a kayak shows the various harpoons and other implements of a seal hunter. Inuit men first made models like this for their children to play with. Later they gave them to European whalers and sealers in exchange for guns or metal tools.

WALRUS HUNT
As soon as Europeans arrived in Canada, they started killing seals. Huge numbers of walruses were shot from boats for their oil, tusks, and leather.

NASTY PICK
Seals have thin skulls. Sealers in the Arctic used picks like this to kill their prey with a quick blow to the head.

GRIZZLY TRADE
These sealers are hacking tusks out of walruses' heads. Walruses were the first seals to be hunted commercially, because they gather in huge herds. When there were almost none left, the sealers turned to grey seals. These are much smaller, but they still contain a lot of valuable oil.

LAST MOMENTS
The killing of harp seals in Canada for their fur became an international controversy. Many people think the hunt is cruel and wasteful. The seals are clubbed on the head, and pups are often killed in front of their mothers. Hunters only take the fur and leave the body.

WILD GRAFFITI
Conservation and animal welfare groups campaigned to end the harp seal hunt. This worker is spraying a pup with dye. This will make its fur worthless to hunters, who may spare it. Film of the seal hunt was shown on TV all over the world.

Purse made from seal fur

MONEY TALKS
Pressure from conservationists led the European Community to ban harp and hooded seal products. Many Canadians are very bitter about this. They claim that the seals are not endangered and should be killed because they eat valuable fish.

Harp seal pup

Myths and legends

THE BEAUTY AND MYSTERY of whales and seals have captured imaginations for centuries. Dolphins feature in the art and myths of most sea-faring nations, and there are many stories of dolphins saving drowning people or helping fishermen to catch fish. Some of these stories are true, and it is often hard to tell myth from fact. Killing dolphins is forbidden in many countries, and the ancient Greeks thought it was as bad as murdering a person. The people of the Amazon say that during fiestas, river dolphins come to shore dressed as men and woo pretty girls. In the Middle Ages, there were all sorts of legends surrounding the narwhal's amazing tusk (pp. 36–37). Strandings of whales are also mentioned in many medieval stories. The dead giants were seen as good or bad omens (p. 56).

GOLD KILLER
This gold killer whale box was carved by Bill Reid. He is part Haida, from the west coast of Canada. The Haida tell stories of the evil ocean people, who used killer whales as canoes. One day they turned a Haida chief into a killer whale. Now this whale protects the Haida from the attacks of the ocean people.

FLIPPER, KING OF THE SEA
The first whale to become a TV star was Flipper, a bottlenose dolphin. When people were in trouble and needed rescuing, Flipper was always there to save the day. Flipper's special friend was a young boy.

Silver coin from Greek colony of Syracuse, 480–479 B.C.

DOLPHIN COINS
There are many ancient Greek and Roman tales and legends about dolphins. One Roman story tells of a boy who was swimming along when a dolphin came up beneath him. The dolphin took him for a ride before pushing him back to the beach. Soon everyone in the village – even the grown-ups – were swimming and playing with the friendly dolphin.

Roman coin from 2nd century B.C.

NEPTUNE'S FRIEND
In this ancient Roman mosaic from a villa in North Africa, a dolphin is carrying Neptune's trident. Neptune was the god of the sea, the Roman version of the Greek god Poseidon. Here he is shown as part horse, part fish, and part man.

Eros, the ancient Greek god of love

Dolphin

STARSTRUCK
This terracotta figure shows Eros, the Greek god of love, riding a dolphin. In one Greek myth, the god Orion is carried into the sky on the back of a dolphin. The gods gave him three stars, which became the constellation Orion's Belt.

BOY AND DOLPHIN
Solitary dolphins around the world seem to seek out human company. They often develop special relationships with certain people and spend hours playing with them. Through history there are many stories of dolphins rescuing drowning people. Some of them are probably true.

Statue of boy and dolphin by English artist David Wynne (born 1926)

STOMACH FULL
In real life, Jonah could never have survived for three days in the belly of a whale (p. 12). There would be no air to breathe and he would suffocate in no time. There is a story of a 19th-century whaler who was swallowed by a sperm whale and found alive when the whale was killed several hours later. Could this incredible story be true?

SEAL STORIES
In many seal legends, the seal disguises itself as a person. In the Orkney Islands off the north coast of Scotland, they tell stories of "selchies". These seals come ashore and behave like people. One story tells of a hunter who married a beautiful girl he met on the beach. One day, she found her fur coat, which he had hidden after they met. She put it on, turned into a seal, and swam away. Tragically, her husband later killed her on a hunting trip.

GREEK SEA LION
This fanciful sea lion has the head of a lion, the hooves of a horse, and the tail of a dolphin.

OUT OF THE BIG BLUE
This is the poster for *The Big Blue*, a 1988 film by the French writer and director Luc Besson. It is the story of two divers, each trying to dive deeper than the other. One is cheery and sociable; the other gets on better with dolphins than people. With its superb underwater photography, *The Big Blue* made millions of people interested in dolphins.

Ancient Greek black figure jar with sea lion, 500–470 B.C.

Strandings and whale watching

UNTIL RECENTLY, most people only saw big whales dead on the beach. This is called stranding. A stranded whale always attracts a crowd. Usually the whale has died at sea and washed up on the shore. But every year, many live whales swim out of the water and strand themselves. Why they do this is still a mystery. Rescuers try to save the whales by covering them with wet towels. This keeps them cool and stops their sensitive skins from burning. When the tide comes in, the whales are helped to swim free. But often they head straight back to the beach and strand again. These days, many people head out to sea to watch live whales. This is a growing industry in many countries.

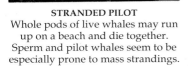

STRANDED PILOT
Whole pods of live whales may run up on a beach and die together. Sperm and pilot whales seem to be especially prone to mass strandings.

Huge baleen whale
stranded on an English beach in 1924

WHY DO THEY DO IT?
People have all sorts of explanations for live stranding. Some say that families strand together because one member of the group is ill. The whales may be lost or disorientated. But because we do not really know how they navigate, this is hard to prove. Strandings of dead whales may be caused by pollution (pp. 58–59), which weakens resistance to disease. Recent "die-offs" of dolphins in the Mediterranean and off the east coast of North America support this theory.

The Stranded Whale, a woodblock print by the Japanese artist Kuniyoshi, about 1851

SAVED, LIVE ON TELEVISION
When winter approaches and the water begins to freeze, whales can become trapped by the advancing ice (pp. 36–37). In 1988, an international rescue was organized to save three gray whales trapped in the Arctic. Inuit workers kept the breathing hole open with chainsaws, while the whole world watched on television. Finally, Russian icebreaker ships cleared a safe path to the sea.

ROYAL FISHES
Since the 14th century, all whales stranded in Britain have officially belonged to the king or queen and are called "Fishes Royal". This pleased Elizabeth I, who was fond of whale meat. In recent years, all strandings were reported to the coast guard. Because of these laws, Britain has kept very good stranding records.

CROWD PULLER
On land, a dead whale's blubber insulates its body, so it warms up and decomposes fast. This is very smelly. The carcass becomes bloated with gases which make the whale more round. This huge sperm whale stranded on a Dutch beach in 1601. The local people thought it was an evil omen.

Watching whales

Around the world, there are many places to go whale watching. In some countries this is becoming a bigger industry than whaling ever was. In Japan and Norway, trips are led by ex-whalers. The gray whales in California are so friendly you can touch them from your canoe. In South Africa, it is forbidden to approach whales in boats, so people watch them from the shore. One town has a "whale crier" whose job is to let people know which bay the whales are in.

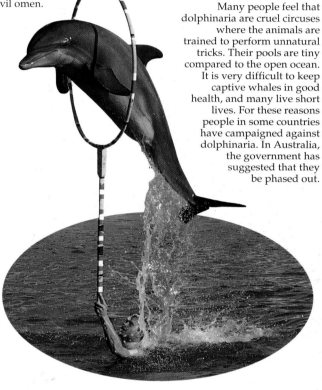

PERFORMING ANIMAL
Many people feel that dolphinaria are cruel circuses where the animals are trained to perform unnatural tricks. Their pools are tiny compared to the open ocean. It is very difficult to keep captive whales in good health, and many live short lives. For these reasons people in some countries have campaigned against dolphinaria. In Australia, the government has suggested that they be phased out.

CLOSE TO A KILLER
Dolphinaria are marine parks where people can come and see dolphins or killer whales. They provide the only chance for many people to see a whale. Our attitude to whales has changed partly because so many people have been able to enjoy them close up.

WHOAH!
Imagine watching a humpback leap right beside your boat. In some places whale watching is big business. Many boats provide spaces for scientists who can study the whales at the same time.

Fishing and pollution

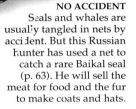

NO ACCIDENT
Seals and whales are usually tangled in nets by accident. But this Russian hunter has used a net to catch a rare Baikal seal (p. 63). He will sell the meat for food and the fur to make coats and hats.

NOW THAT MOST countries have stopped hunting them, the biggest threats whales and seals face are fishing and pollution. Every year, hundreds of thousands of whales and seals are drowned when they become tangled in fishing nets. The fishermen often view the mammals as pests. In countries like Norway and Canada, overfishing by people has reduced fish stocks. But the fishermen blame seals and whales for the problem and campaign for hunts to keep their numbers down (p. 53). The oceans are being used as a dustbin for the poisonous chemicals produced by industry. Once toxic chemicals have been released into the sea, it is impossible to recover them. They are invisible but deadly. Whales and seals are particularly at risk because many pollutants collect in their fat.

INTO THE AIR AND SEA
Most methods of making paper produce highly poisonous chemicals. This is one of the paper mills that dump their waste into the world's largest freshwater lake, Lake Baikal in Russia. It is home to the endangered Baikal seal.

DOLPHIN TRAP
Trawlers catch fish by dragging nets like this one through the water. When two boats trawl together, the nets are so big that a whole school of dolphins could swim in and not be able to get out.

SWIMMING IN OIL
When a sea otter (p. 7) gets covered in oil, its fur becomes matted. The animal has trouble keeping warm and may die of cold. In a desperate attempt to lick itself clean, the otter will also swallow poisonous oil. Hundreds of rare sea otters were hurt or killed in the *Exxon Valdez* oil spill in Alaska in 1989. Oil damages habitats and poisons food supplies. Oil poured into the Persian Gulf during the Gulf War of 1991 harmed the sea grass beds where dugongs feed. No one knows what the long-term effects of such huge spills will be.

WHALE-SIZED MESS
Everyone is horrified when an oil tanker is wrecked and pours its oil into the sea. Clean-up teams can usually only recover a small part of the oil. It is much more important to prevent such disasters from happening in the first place.

INVISIBLE POISONS
Many poisonous chemicals are dumped into the sea. Some are pesticides such as DDT. These are passed up the food chain and concentrated in the bodies of predators like seals and whales. We now know that female whales pass these pollutants directly to their young through their milk.

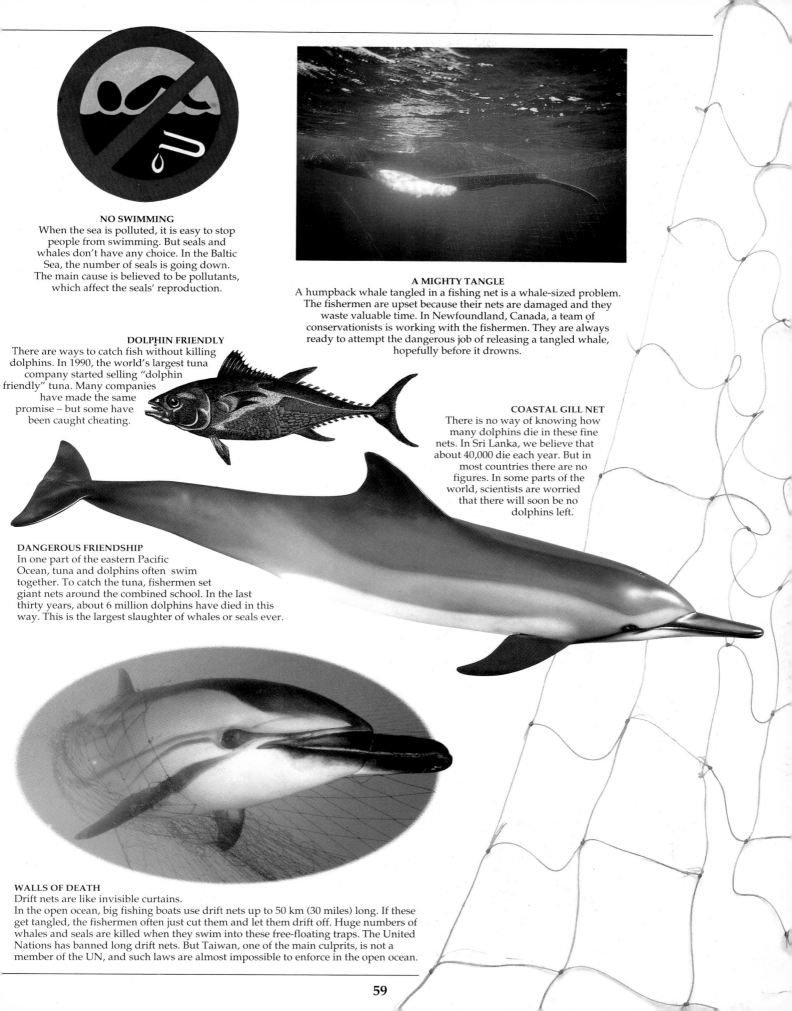

NO SWIMMING
When the sea is polluted, it is easy to stop people from swimming. But seals and whales don't have any choice. In the Baltic Sea, the number of seals is going down. The main cause is believed to be pollutants, which affect the seals' reproduction.

A MIGHTY TANGLE
A humpback whale tangled in a fishing net is a whale-sized problem. The fishermen are upset because their nets are damaged and they waste valuable time. In Newfoundland, Canada, a team of conservationists is working with the fishermen. They are always ready to attempt the dangerous job of releasing a tangled whale, hopefully before it drowns.

DOLPHIN FRIENDLY
There are ways to catch fish without killing dolphins. In 1990, the world's largest tuna company started selling "dolphin friendly" tuna. Many companies have made the same promise – but some have been caught cheating.

COASTAL GILL NET
There is no way of knowing how many dolphins die in these fine nets. In Sri Lanka, we believe that about 40,000 die each year. But in most countries there are no figures. In some parts of the world, scientists are worried that there will soon be no dolphins left.

DANGEROUS FRIENDSHIP
In one part of the eastern Pacific Ocean, tuna and dolphins often swim together. To catch the tuna, fishermen set giant nets around the combined school. In the last thirty years, about 6 million dolphins have died in this way. This is the largest slaughter of whales or seals ever.

WALLS OF DEATH
Drift nets are like invisible curtains.
In the open ocean, big fishing boats use drift nets up to 50 km (30 miles) long. If these get tangled, the fishermen often just cut them and let them drift off. Huge numbers of whales and seals are killed when they swim into these free-floating traps. The United Nations has banned long drift nets. But Taiwan, one of the main culprits, is not a member of the UN, and such laws are almost impossible to enforce in the open ocean.

Studying sea mammals

W‍E STILL KNOW VERY LITTLE about the lives of seals and whales. The first information on anatomy came from cutting up dead animals, and the contents of the stomach or ovaries gave clues on diet or reproduction. More recently, many new techniques that do not harm animals have been developed. Some involve photography; others require small tissue samples. Whales live in a world of sound (pp. 26–27), and an underwater microphone can be used to find, follow, and even count them. One of the hardest questions to answer is: "How many whales are there?" Scientists and mathematicians have been working on this problem for three decades. But we still have only rough estimates for the size of most populations.

French engraving from 19th century showing scientists studying a model whale

JACQUES COUSTEAU
This French adventurer has made many popular films and books about life under the sea.

DNA FINGERPRINTING
Scientists can now use a small piece of skin or muscle to identify an individual animal. They do this by examining the animal's DNA, its genetic material. The result, a DNA fingerprint, looks something like a bar code. Scientists can then use the bands to identify close relatives, for example an animal's parents or sisters.

Crown

Birth line

First year ring

Rings for every year's growth

Pulp cavity

Root

Cross-section of harbour porpoise's tooth

WHALES ALIVE
One of the best ways to study whales in their element is from small sailing boats (motor boats can make a lot of noise). Researchers take photos to identify individuals. Microphones left under the water follow the whales' vocalizations. The whales' social life can be pieced together from all this information.

Nicks caused by parasites, fights, or collisions with boats

HERE'S MY I.D.
Every humpback whale has a unique black-and-white pattern on the underside of its tail. Thousands of humpbacks have been photographed and their patterns recorded. Every time a whale is sighted, its pattern is checked against the catalogue to see if it has been spotted before. This allows scientists to count populations, follow whales as they migrate, and learn who they spend their time with.

READING A TOOTH
A whale's tooth has rings just like a tree. A new ring is laid down every year. After cutting a tooth in half and etching it with chemicals, a researcher can count the layers and calculate the whale's age. The appearance of the layers also gives clues to how well fed or healthy the whale was from one year to the next.

Scratches from other dolphin's teeth

SCRATCHED AND SCARRED
Whales collect scratches and scars as they swim through life. These tell-tale marks can be used to identify individual animals. This is easier with old whales, like this 25-year-old bottlenose dolphin, which have more scars. The problem is that marks may change, which makes identification uncertain!

EARLY DISSECTION

Much of our early information on whales comes from the whaling industry. Early whalers and scientists recorded every conceivable piece of information on the gigantic corpses. Now most of the questions that remain can only be answered by studying live animals.

ON THE PULSE

This acoustic transmitter broadcasts the heartbeat. This changes drastically when the animal goes for a deep dive.

Sensor which shows how deep seal is diving and how fast it is swimming

Radio antenna

Remnants of moulted fur

Used satellite tag with moulted fur

SATELLITE TAG

When the animal surfaces, the data stored in this transmitter is beamed to a satellite and on to the lab.

VHF tag which sends out a radio signal

Acoustic tag

Tags for tracking

How do you follow a seal or a whale without getting wet? One way is to attach a tag to its body. This can then send back information on where the animal goes, how fast it swims, or how deep it dives. The most sophisticated tags send their signals to satellites. These tags are expensive, but their signals can be tracked anywhere in the world.

SEEING UNDER THE SEA

This computer-generated map shows the movements of a tagged elephant seal. One seal swam an incredible 2,650 km (1,640 miles) in 70 days. This seal is looking for food along the edge of the continental shelf. Every vertical white line is a dive.

Tip of Antarctic continent

Sea level

Path of seal

Sea bottom over continental shelf

Edge of continental shelf

Deep ocean bottom

FOLLOWING HIS NOSE

Attaching tags to seals or whales is not an easy job. This big male elephant seal (pp. 40–41) has a tag glued to his head. When he moults in the spring, the tag will fall off with his old fur. Other tags are shot into the skin of whales. But some people think this is cruel.

Save the whale!

STAMP DUTY
Developing countries are becoming aware of conservation problems. These stamps from Sri Lanka show some of the country's marine mammals.

THE FUTURE OF WHALES and seals depends on people from all over the world getting together and co-operating. The seas are a common resource. How should they be used? Will it ever be possible to catch whales humanely and without hunting them to extinction? Can we develop whale tourism instead? Is keeping dolphins in captivity cruel (p. 57)? How can we control pollution and the use of fishing nets (pp. 58–59)? Even agreeing which species are endangered is difficult. Many countries have different views on all these questions – usually for their own reasons. Because whales migrate, they do not just belong to the countries that want to hunt them. The only way forward is by international co-operation, rational discussion, and good science. People are becoming more aware of the problems, but this is only the first step. Good intentions must be followed by real action and commitment. Only then can we safeguard the future of these magnificent animals.

Whale drawing by Liam Bleach, age 5

Blue whale drawn by Domoniqua Douglas, age 5

STARTING EARLY
The best way to change attitudes to whales and seals is to get children interested at an early age. These days most children know a lot about environmental issues. Often they have to teach their parents!

Distinctive short, rounded snout

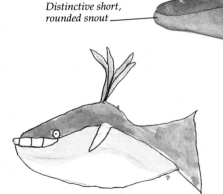

Whale drawing by Giuseppe Paese, age 6

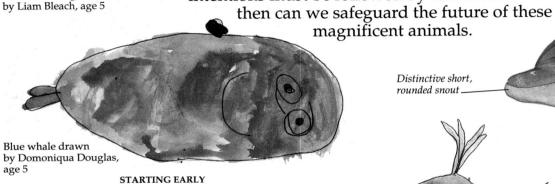

ABORIGINAL WHALING
With a leap from his wooden boat, a man drives a long bamboo pole into a whale. Only two villages in Indonesia still hunt whales in this way. Elsewhere in the world, a few whales are still caught in traditional ways in Tonga, Alaska, and Bequia in the Caribbean. Hundreds of narwhals and belugas are killed every year in Greenland (pp. 36–37).

MASS SLAUGHTER
In the Færoe Islands between Scotland and Iceland, whole pods of pilot whales are still hunted. The whales are driven ashore and killed. There has been an international outcry against the hunt, and the hunters have been portrayed as cruel. But because the complaints come from outside the islands, the Færoese have become more determined than ever to continue the yearly hunt.

Endangered species

A few species of whale and seal are close to disappearing forever. There are few blue whales left in the southern oceans (pp. 20–21). The areas they roam are so vast that they may not be able to find a mate! Gray whales were almost extinct by 1946. Now the California population has gone up to about 20,000.

RIGHT WHALES
The right whales are all threatened by extinction. The rarest of all, the bowhead, is still hunted in small numbers in Alaska (p. 49). Slow-moving northern right whales are often killed when they are hit by boats. One bright spot is South Africa, where southern right whales are becoming more common.

AMAZON RIVER DOLPHIN
This Amazon River dolphin was killed by a fisherman. Several species of river dolphin are on the verge of extinction (p. 33). A dam has divided the Indus River species into two populations. Only a miracle will save the Chinese river dolphin. There are less than 200 left in the entire Changjiang (Yangtze River) system.

LAKE BAIKAL SEAL
We now know what needs to be done to save some species, like this Baikal seal. It is threatened by pollution, and will only survive if paper mills stop pouring poisons into Lake Baikal (p. 58). For many other species of seal, there are no easy answers. The numbers of certain species, like the Steller's sea lion (pp. 23, 30–31) and the southern elephant seal (pp. 40–41), are going down. No one is sure why this is happening, or what to do to save them.

SET FREE
The welfare of captive animals is now an issue in some countries (p. 57). Many dolphinaria were built decades ago and no longer meet new standards. These dolphins, Silver and Missie, used to live in an underground dolphinarium in Brighton in England. When the old building was sold, the new owners decided to return the animals to the wild.

Pale grey colour, darker on back and turning to white on belly

BACK TO THE OPEN OCEAN
After months of planning, the two dolphins were carried in slings into an aeroplane and flown to an island in the Caribbean. They spent several months in a fenced-off lagoon learning how to catch live fish. Then they were set free.

The bottlenose dolphin is the largest dolphin, growing up to 4 m (13 ft) long and weighing as much as 650 kg (1,450 lb)

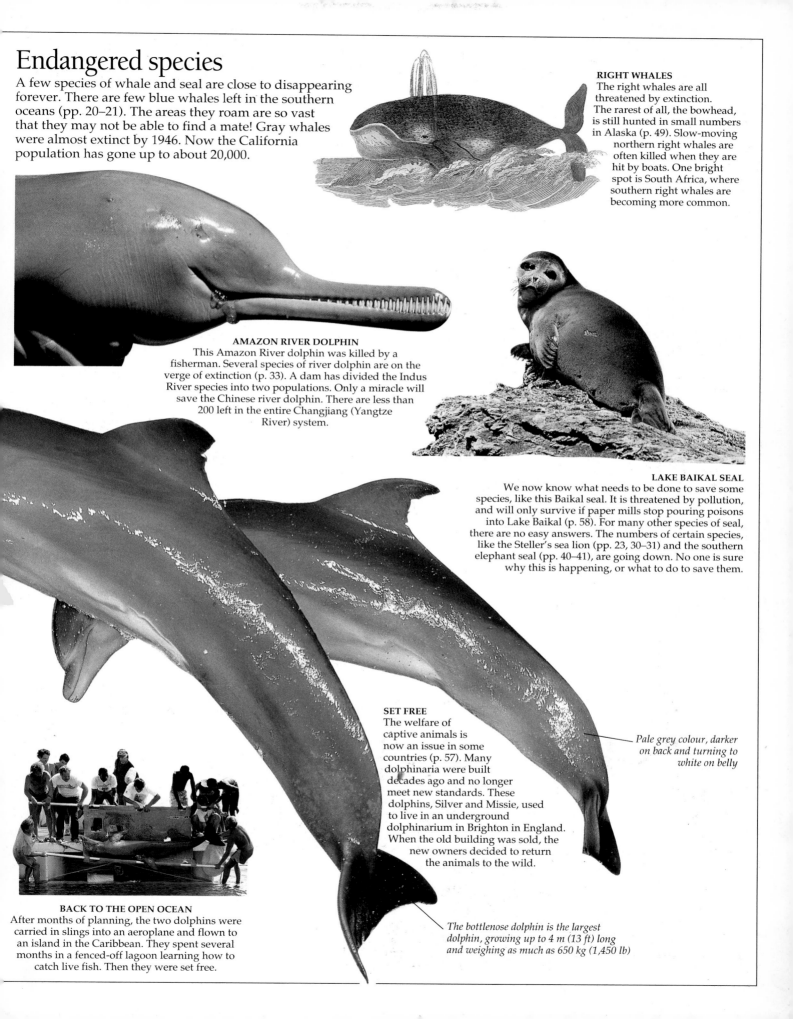

Did you know?

AMAZING FACTS

Blue whale calves have the fastest growth rate of any animal. In the first six months, they gain 4 kg (9 lb) an hour, and grow 4 cm (1.5 in) longer a day!

The huge head of a sperm whale

The sperm whale has the biggest head of any living creature on land or in the sea. It eats up to 1 tonne (1 ton) of squid each day, and is also the only animal with a gullet big enough to fit a human!

Harp seals

Harp seals never live on land, but, for two weeks each year, they live on the Arctic ice for breeding. They then quickly head back out to sea for safety.

The right whale was named by whalers because it was the "right" whale for hunting. It is slow, easy to approach, lives close to the shore, floats when killed, is found in temperate waters and gives a high yield of oil. As a result, its numbers dropped to just 400 animals, but they have been protected since 1935 and there are now thought to be around 2,000.

Humpback whales are important colonies for barnacles. They carry up to 450 kg (990 lbs) of them on their bodies.

Blue whales were nearly wiped out by hunting. At the peak in 1931, 29,000 were killed in one season, from a pre-hunting total population of around 200,000. Hunting was banned in 1966, and the population now stands at around 15,000.

Killer whales don't kill people as they rarely come across them and, even if they did, humans have too little blubber to make a good meal.

When Inuit hunters found ivory arrowheads 130-200 years old embedded in the flesh of a bowhead whale, scientists began to test bowheads and found many were over 100 years old, and some were 200! On average, however, it is thought that whales live 50-70 years, with the larger whales living the longest.

Intelligence is difficult to measure, but scientists can measure the size of an animal's brain by comparing the volume of its brain with surface area of its body. This is called its EQ. Humans have an EQ of 7.4 and chimpanzees have an EQ of 2.5. The cetacean with the highest EQ is the bottlenose dolphin with a rating of 5.6.

Many cetaceans like to give their calves piggy-back rides while they swim along. Some porpoises even have rough patches of skin on their backs to help the calves grip onto their bodies.

A whale's heartbeat rate slows down by half during a deep dive to slow down the consumption of precious oxygen supplies. Whales can also store oxygen in their muscles for use when diving for long periods.

A killer whale spyhopping

Many cetaceans like to raise their heads straight up out of the water and take a look around. Sometimes they even turn in a circle before slipping back into the water. This is called spyhopping.

Scientists can work out the age of some whales by looking at their teeth. These are made up of layers, like the growth rings of a tree, with about a year's growth for each layer.

Elephant seals gather together in huge colonies to breed. Sadly the beaches become so crowded that up to 20 per cent of the seal pups are crushed to death by the enormous adults.

An elephant seal colony

QUESTIONS AND ANSWERS

Q How are sea mammals affected by pollution in the water?

A Scientists examining whales have found that they absorb pollutants. In particular, beluga whales in the Gulf of St Lawrence, Canada, have been discovered with such high levels of chemicals in their bodies that, when they die, they have to be treated as toxic waste. These pollutants inevitably affect the animals' health.

A pygmy sperm whale logging

Q How do cetaceans sleep and breathe at the same time?

A Cetaceans sleep in different ways. Some whales lie motionless, just below the surface of the water, with part of their head, and sometimes a fin, exposed. This is called logging. Dolphins group together and take it in turns to dive and sleep for short periods, resting just half their brain at a time. Dall's porpoise, however, never seems to sleep at all.

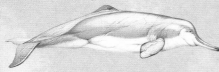

The Baiji, a river dolphin from China

Q There are many species of cetaceans that are under threat, but which is the rarest of them all?

A One of the rarest creatures on Earth is a river dolphin from China, called the Baiji. The Baiji is number two on the list of the most endangered species in the world. It is a very shy animal, and only 150-200 Baiji are believed to be still living in the Yangstze River. It is threatened by injury from boats and pollution.

Humpback whales bubble netting

A humpback pushes her calf to the surface

Q Whale calves are born in the water, so is there a danger they will drown before they take their first breath?

A There is a danger that when a baby whale is born it will not know what to do, but the mother whale will help her calf by pushing it up towards the surface.

Q Do marine mammals drink sea water?

A No, marine mammals get their water from their food and from moisture in the air they breathe. They have especially powerful kidneys to get rid of the salt they inevitably swallow.

A humpback whale scoops up salt water but does not drink it.

Q How many dolphins are killed each year in fishing nets?

A In the 1960s it was thought that around 100,000 dolphins were being killed each year in fishing nets. Better fishing practices have improved the situation dramatically and it is believed that this number dropped to around 4,000 dolphins by 2000.

Q What should I do if I found a live stranded whale or dolphin?

A Note down any helpful details, such as the size and species of the animal, or any distinguishing features, and call the police or the coastguard, who will contact the local rescue team. Until help arrives, try to keep the animal cool and moist with seaweed or wet towels, taking care to avoid the eyes and blowhole. Do not try and drag or move the animal or you will harm it.

Record Breakers

BIGGEST CETACEAN
The biggest blue whale ever recorded was a male found in the Shetland Islands in 1926, which measured 32.64 m (107 ft 1 in).

SMALLEST CETACEAN
The dwarf sperm whale is 2.1-2.7 m (7-9 ft) long and weighs just 135-275 kg (300-600 lb).

FASTEST SWIMMER
The fastest marine mammals are Dall's porpoise and the killer whale, which can both reach speeds of 56 kph (35 mph).

HUNGRIEST WHALE
An adult blue whale needs to eat 1.5-million calories a day – that's about 40-million krill.

BIGGEST CETACEAN TEETH
Sperm whales have the biggest teeth of all the cetaceans, at 20 cm (8 inches) long. Right whales don't have teeth, but they do have the longest baleen plates, which can be up to 4.3 m (14 feet) long.

Who's who?

WHILE SOME CETACEANS ARE VERY DISTINCTIVE, others are much more difficult to identify. Below is an outline of the characteristics of each of the main groups with illustrations showing clearly the features that set them apart. This should help you to begin to work out the species you are looking at. A scale drawing gives the true size of each example.

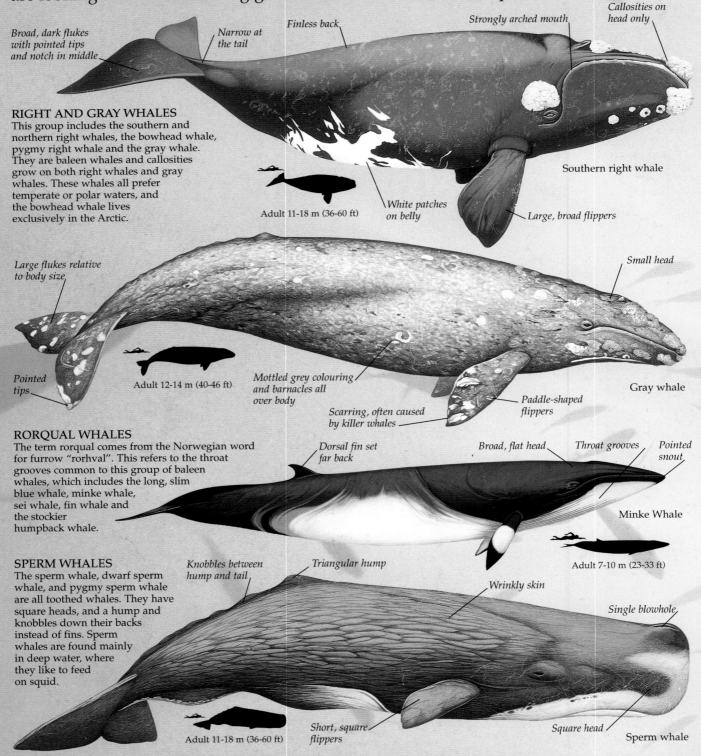

Broad, dark flukes with pointed tips and notch in middle

Narrow at the tail

Finless back

Strongly arched mouth

Callosities on head only

RIGHT AND GRAY WHALES
This group includes the southern and northern right whales, the bowhead whale, pygmy right whale and the gray whale. They are baleen whales and callosities grow on both right whales and gray whales. These whales all prefer temperate or polar waters, and the bowhead whale lives exclusively in the Arctic.

Adult 11-18 m (36-60 ft)

White patches on belly

Southern right whale

Large, broad flippers

Large flukes relative to body size

Small head

Adult 12-14 m (40-46 ft)

Pointed tips

Mottled grey colouring and barnacles all over body

Scarring, often caused by killer whales

Paddle-shaped flippers

Gray whale

RORQUAL WHALES
The term rorqual comes from the Norwegian word for furrow "rorhval". This refers to the throat grooves common to this group of baleen whales, which includes the long, slim blue whale, minke whale, sei whale, fin whale and the stockier humpback whale.

Dorsal fin set far back

Broad, flat head

Throat grooves

Pointed snout

Minke Whale

Adult 7-10 m (23-33 ft)

SPERM WHALES
The sperm whale, dwarf sperm whale, and pygmy sperm whale are all toothed whales. They have square heads, and a hump and knobbles down their backs instead of fins. Sperm whales are found mainly in deep water, where they like to feed on squid.

Knobbles between hump and tail

Triangular hump

Wrinkly skin

Single blowhole

Adult 11-18 m (36-60 ft)

Short, square flippers

Square head

Sperm whale

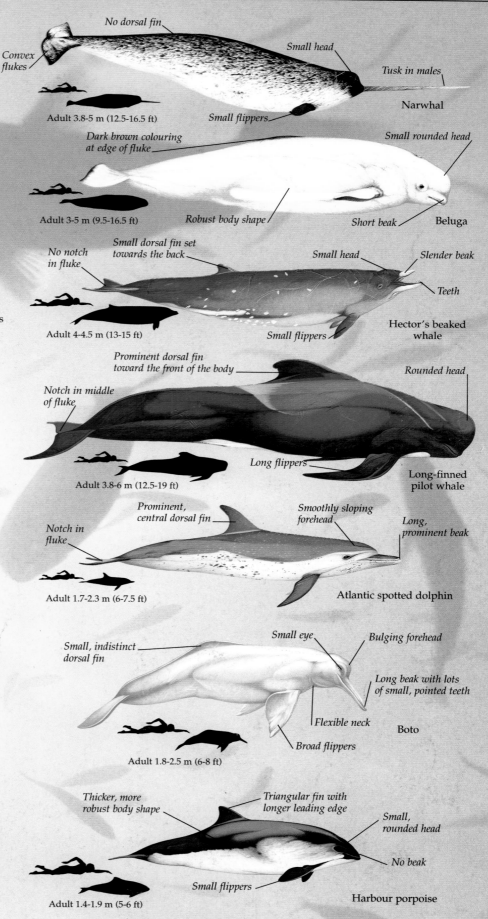

NARWHAL AND BELUGA

Although the narwhal and beluga are related, they each have very distinctive and unusual appearances. Both species live in the cold, remote waters of the Arctic and subarctic, where they are common. Both the narwhal and the beluga are similar in size, are toothed and have thick blubber to protect them from the cold. Unlike other whales, they are both able to change their facial expression. Beluga calves are born dark brown and turn white as they mature.

No dorsal fin

Convex flukes

Small head

Tusk in males

Narwhal

Adult 3.8-5 m (12.5-16.5 ft)

Small flippers

Dark brown colouring at edge of fluke

Small rounded head

Adult 3-5 m (9.5-16.5 ft)

Robust body shape

Short beak

Beluga

BEAKED WHALES

Beaked whales are rarely seen because they live in deep water far from land. They can range in size from 4 m (13 ft) to nearly 13 m (43 ft). Most males have very distinctive teeth, with just two or four teeth in the lower jaw and none in the upper jaw. The teeth can usually be seen when the jaws are closed and are sometimes very large. Most females have no teeth at all.

No notch in fluke

Small dorsal fin set towards the back

Small head

Slender beak

Teeth

Adult 4-4.5 m (13-15 ft)

Small flippers

Hector's beaked whale

BLACKFISH

This family of smaller toothed whales, which includes the killer whale and the long- and short-finned pilot whales, is more closely related to dolphins than whales. But blackfish do not look like dolphins and most prefer deep water. These are mostly very gregarious whales that live together in strong groups.

Prominent dorsal fin toward the front of the body

Rounded head

Notch in middle of fluke

Long flippers

Adult 3.8-6 m (12.5-19 ft)

Long-finned pilot whale

OCEANIC DOLPHINS

Oceanic dolphins can be divided into two main groups: those with prominent beaks and those that have short rounded beaks. There is a wide variety of colouring, patterns and body shapes between the species. While some have a very streamlined body, others are more robust in shape.

Prominent, central dorsal fin

Smoothly sloping forehead

Long, prominent beak

Notch in fluke

Adult 1.7-2.3 m (6-7.5 ft)

Atlantic spotted dolphin

RIVER DOLPHINS

River dolphins can be found in the largest rivers of Asia and South America: the Boto in the Orinoco and the Amazon of South America, the Baiji in the Yangtze in China, plus species found in the Indus and the Ganges of Asia. The different species are not related but they are similar. They are all small, slow swimmers with long, narrow beaks and are almost blind.

Small, indistinct dorsal fin

Small eye

Bulging forehead

Long beak with lots of small, pointed teeth

Flexible neck

Boto

Broad flippers

Adult 1.8-2.5 m (6-8 ft)

PORPOISES

Porpoises live mainly along the coast but can also be found in rivers and out in open sea. Their numbers are on the decline because they often get entangled in fishing nets. They are some of the smallest cetaceans and, unlike dolphins, are quite shy. Most species tend to avoid people. They are difficult to identify because little of their body is usually seen above the surface of the water.

Thicker, more robust body shape

Triangular fin with longer leading edge

Small, rounded head

No beak

Small flippers

Adult 1.4-1.9 m (5-6 ft)

Harbour porpoise

Find out more

I<small>T IS POSSIBLE TO SEE WHALES</small>, dolphins, porpoises and other marine mammals in many parts of the world, but to increase your chances of finding them it helps to do some research first. Commercial trips are often the best way to see whales because the organizers will know the seasonal movements of the different species in the area, the most likely places to find them, and will have the most up-to-the-minute local information.

NEW ZEALAND
Sperm whales, dolphins and seals can be seen off the coast of Kaikoura, in New Zealand. This whale is showing the vertical fluking that is distinctive in sperm whales and makes them relatively easy to identify (see box right).

WHERE TO SEE WHALES
The map below shows some of the locations around the world where you are most likely to see a variety of whales, dolphins or porpoises.

Disko Bay (Greenland)
Hofn (Iceland)
Lofoten Islands (Norway)
Glacier Bay (Alaska)
Inner Hebrides (Scotland)
Vancouver Island (Canada)
NORTH AMERICA
Newfoundland (Canada)
West coast of Ireland
EUROPE
Southern California (USA)
Gulf of St Lawrence (Canada)
Azores (Portugal)
ASIA
Baja California (Mexico)
New England (USA)
Shikoku Island (Japan)
Bahamas
Canary Islands (Spain)
Ogasawara (Japan)
Hawaii (USA)
AFRICA
PACIFIC OCEAN
Trincomalee (Sri Lanka)
SOUTH AMERICA
ATLANTIC OCEAN
AUSTRALASIA
PACIFIC OCEAN
INDIAN OCEAN
Hervey Bay (Australia)
Monkey Mia (Australia)
Valdes Peninsular (Argentina)
Hermanus (South Africa)
Logan's Beach (Australia)
Kaikoura (New Zealand)

MEXICO
These tourists near San Ignacio, in Mexico, are able to stroke a grey whale, but it is important that groups of boats do not get too close or the whales may feel trapped.

FREDERICK SOUND, ALASKA
From June to September, tourists can see humpback whales off the coast of Alaska. The whales feed there during the summer months, then they head off on the long journey south to breed in the warmer waters off the coast of Mexico.

IDENTIFYING WHALES

Wᴴᴱɴ ʏᴏᴜ ᴅᴏ ꜱᴇᴇ ᴀɴ ᴀɴɪᴍᴀʟ in the water, it is not always easy to identify – even for experts – as many species look alike and much of the body will be under the water. Observe the animal closely to get as much information as possible and take notes. If you can, make a sketch or take photographs of the shape of the tail and fins. Notes on the following points will help you identify the species later on:

- Size
- Any unusual features (e.g. tusk)
- The position shape and colour of the dorsal fin
- Body and head shape
- Colour and markings
- The height and shape of any blow
- Shape and markings of tail flukes
- Behaviour on the surface and dive sequence
- Style of breaching
- Number of animals in group
- Habitat
- Geographical location

Dorsal fin of a
bottle nose dolphin

Dorsal fin of a
killer whale

DORSAL FIN
Note whether the animal has a dorsal fin or hump. What shape is the fin? Is it big or small, curved or pointed? Where is it on the animal's body?

USEFUL WEBSITES

- Cetacean Society International:
  www.csiwhalesalive.org
- International Dolphin Watch:
  www.IDW.org
- The Whale and Dolphin Conservation Society:
  www.wdcs.org
- Greenpeace, for information on conservation issues:
  www.greenpeace.org
- WhaleNet, an interactive educational website:
  whale.wheelock.edu

TAIL FLUKES AND PATTERNS
The tail flukes of different species of whales are often distinctive, so look at their shape and note whether there is a notch. In humpback whales, the unique patterns of the markings have enabled scientists to identify thousands of individuals.

DIVE SEQUENCE
The dive sequence of the sperm whale is distinctive because it dives to great depths. It starts by lifting its head out of the water for a final breath. Up to two-thirds of the body can be seen above the surface.

The body straightens, and after gently arching its back, the whale may disappear. It then accelerates forward and reappears slightly as it arches its back again. With the arched back high out of the water, the rounded hump and the distinctive knobbly back of the whale can be seen clearly.

Finally, the flukes and near third of the body are thrown high up into the air and then drop vertically, barely disturbing the water's surface.

Places to visit

THE NATURAL HISTORY MUSEUM, CROMWELL ROAD, LONDON
Displays on marine mammals, including real animal skeletons and life-size models.

WHALE WATCHING IN GREAT BRITAIN
A variety of cetaceans, and also seals and sea lions, can be seen in the waters off Great Britain. Consult the Whale and Dolphin Conservation Society website for details of what to see where.

THE NATIONAL SEAL SANCTUARY, GWEEK, NEAR HELSTON, CORNWALL
A rescue and rehabilitation centre for seals with resident seals and sea lions.

SCOTTISH SEA-LIFE AND MARINE SANCTUARY, LOCH CRERAN, OBAN, ARGYLL
A rescue and rehabilitation facility for common and grey seal pups.

BREACHING BEHAVIOUR
The way a cetacean breaches can also help to identify it. The humpback whale, for example, often lifts two-thirds of its body out of the water as it leaps. Note how often the animal breaches and whether it twists as it jumps. Also look to see if it lifts its body out vertically or at a shallow angle.

Glossary

ALBINO An animal that appears white because it is lacking colour in its skin, hair and eyes.

AMBERGRIS Hard, waxy substance found in the gut of the sperm whale. Highly valued in the perfume trade in the past.

BALEEN/BALEEN PLATES Thin, comb-like plates that hang from the upper jaw of some of the large whales. Used to strain small creatures, like krill, from the sea water.

BALEEN WHALES Sub-order of whales with baleen plates.

BEACH RUBBING Rubbing the body against stones in shallow water.

BEAK The pointed jaw of cetaceans such as bottlenose dolphins. A beak is also known as a snout.

BLOW The cloud of spray, also called a spout, that shoots into the air when a cetacean exhales from its blow-hole.

BLOW-HOLE The nostril (or nostrils) on the top of a cetacean's head. The only body opening through which a cetacean can breathe.

BLUBBER The thick layer of insulating fat that lies just under the skin of most marine mammals.

BOW-RIDE To ride on the wave created at the bow of a ship, boat or even a large whale as it cuts its way through the water.

BOTTLING Sleeping at the surface of the water with the nostrils poking out. A term used to describe the behaviour of seals.

BREACHING Leaping out of the water and making a loud splash on re-entry.

BUBBLE NETTING Blowing bubbles under the water to create a spiral of bubbles which herds fish together. A fishing method used by humpback whales.

BULL The name given to an adult male marine mammal.

CALF Young cetacean that is still being fed and cared for by its mother.

CALLOSITIES The rough skin or lumpy growths found on the heads of right whales. The colouring and appearance of these growths is caused by barnacles, lice and parasitic worms that live on them.

A humpback whale blowing

CETACEAN A marine mammal belonging to the order Cetacea, which includes all whales, dolphins and porpoises.

CODA A pattern of slow clicking noises used by whales, such as sperm whales and killer whales, either for communication or perhaps to stun their prey. Sometimes referred to as a "click train".

The tail flukes of a right whale

COW The name given to an adult female marine mammal.

DORSAL FIN The raised fin on the back of most cetaceans.

ECHO-LOCATION The system of making sounds and listening to the returning echoes that most cetaceans use to find food and to navigate.

FILTER FEEDERS Animals that feed by extracting food, such as plankton and krill, from the water using baleen plates, gills or beaks as filters.

FLENSING The whaling term for the process of cutting up a whale's blubber and skin.

FLIPPER The front limb of a cetacean.

FLIPPERING To raise a flipper out of the water and slap it deliberately on the surface to make a loud noise. Also known as flipper-slapping.

FLUKE A flat, end part on a cetacean's tail that has no bone.

Krill

FLUKING Lifting the tail, or flukes, up into the air as a cetacean begins to dive.

HERD A group of cetaceans living and working together. Used mainly to describe larger baleen whales.

INUIT The native people of the Arctic regions of Canada and Greenland.

KERATIN Continually growing protein that forms human nails and hair, and the baleen of whales.

KRILL Tiny shrimp-like crustaceans. The principal food for most baleen whales.

Callosities on the head of a right whale

LOBTAILING Slapping the tail flukes hard against the surface of the water, while most of the animal's body lies beneath the surface.

LOGGING Floating motionless at the surface of the water. A form of rest.

MAMMAL A warm-blooded animal that suckles its young.

MELON A raised area on the forehead of many toothed whales, dolphins and porpoises, where it is believed that sounds are focused for echo-location.

MIGRATION A regular journey by an animal from one region to another because of changes in the climate or for breeding and feeding purposes.

ORCA The more common name for the killer whale.

PARASITE An animal or organism that lives off another animal causing it harm.

PECTORAL FINS The front limbs of a cetacean, also called flippers.

PINNIPEDS Animals with fins for feet, such as seals, sea lions and walruses.

PLANKTON Microscopic marine organisms.

A pod of killer whales

POD A group of cetaceans working or living together. A term used mainly to describe the larger toothed whales.

PORPOISING Leaping out of the water and moving forward at speed, behaviour common in dolphins and rare in porpoises.

PREDATOR An animal that preys on other animals for food.

PUP Term used for a young seal, sea lion or walrus.

RESIDENT Staying in the same area all year round.

RORQUAL WHALES From the Norwegian word "rorvhal" meaning "furrow", the name given to the group of whales that have throat grooves.

SADDLE The light patch behind the dorsal fin of some cetaceans.

SCHOOL Collective noun for a group of cetaceans such as dolphins.

SEALING The hunting of seals for their fur, meat and blubber.

SONAR A system of navigation using sound that is used by animals such as cetaceans and bats for echo-location.

SPECIES A group of similar animals that are able to breed amongst themselves.

SPERMACETI ORGAN Large area in the head of sperm whales containing a thick waxy liquid called spermaceti oil.

SPYHOPPING Raising the head out of the water to see what is going on, and then disappearing beneath the surface with very little splash.

A killer whale is a small toothed cetacean

The throat grooves of a humpback whale

STRANDING When a cetacean becomes stranded on land.

THROAT GROOVES Grooves on the throat of some types of baleen whale which allow the throat to expand and take in large quantities of food and water.

TOOTHED WHALES The sub-order of whales with teeth rather than baleen plates.

TRANSIENT Always on the move rather than settled in one place.

TUSK A large protruding tooth.

WAKE-RIDING Riding on the waves created by a moving boat or ship.

WEAN To get an infant mammal used to eating food other than its mother's milk.

WHALEBONE Not a bone, but the traditional name for the tough baleen plates when used as a product of whaling.

WHALE LICE Small, crab-like parasites that live on some species of whale.

WHALING The commercial hunting of whales by people.

A dolphin wake-riding

Index

Acknowledgements

Vassili Papastavrou would like to dedicate this book to Catherine and thank Mel Brooks, Nigel & Jennifer Bonner, Tom Arnbom, Bill Amos, Denise Herzing, Graham Leach, Gill Hartley, Simon Hay and Nick Davies.
Dorling Kindersley would like to thank Jon Kershaw & the staff of Marineland, Antibes, France; Ron Kastelein & the staff of Harderwijk Marine Mammal Park, Holland; Adrian Friday & Ray Symonds at University Museum of Zoology, Cambridge, for skeletons (pp. 12, 13, 23, 25, 36, 40, 43); Bob Headland at Scott Polar Institute, Cambridge, for the harpoon gun (pp. 48–49) & Inuit sculptures (pp. 15, 42); John Ward at the British Antarctic Survey for the krill (p. 25); Arthur Credland at Town Docks Museum, Hull for the whaling artefacts (pp. 46–53); John Shearer for the nets (pp. 56–57); the Sea Mammal Research Unit, Cambridge, esp. Christine Lockyer for the tooth (p. 60) & Kevin Nicholas & Bernie McConnell for the tags (p. 61); Sarah Richardson and the pupils of Townsend Primary School, London (p. 62); Jocelyn Steedman in Vancouver; Helena Spiteri for editorial help; Sharon Spencer, Manisha Patel and Jabu Mahlangu for design help.

Additional photography: Harry Taylor, Natural History Museum, London; Ivor Curzlake, British Museum, London (pp. 2–3, 33 & 54–55); Dave King (pp. 6, 10tl, 32–33 & 62–63) and JerryYoung (p. 7).
Index: Céline Carez

Picture credits
t=top b=bottom m=middle l=left r=right
American Museum of Natural History, New York 20-21; Ancient Art & Architecture Collection 6tl, 36tl, 46tl; Aquarius Library / MGM 54cl; Ardea London Limited / F. Gohier 18tl, 56b; Tom Arnbom 41tl, 41tr; Auscape International / D. Parer & E. Parer-Cook 34cr, 34br; Baleine Blanche French School Afloat /G. Hartley 60c; Barnaby's Picture Library / W. Lüthy 48tl / N.D. Price 51cla; BFl / © Gaumont 1988 55bl; BBC Natural History Unit: Mary Ann Mcdonald 68bl. Bibliothèque Nationale, Paris / Gallimard Jeunesse 12bc; Nigel Bonner 48bl; Bridgeman Art Library / Giraudon 32tl / Private Collection 55tr, 57tl; Staatlich Antikens-ammlung, Munich 2tr; British Museum, London 42tr; Bruce Coleman Limited / Mark Carwardine 71br; / Pacific Stock 68bc; Corbis Stock Market: Amos Nachoum 65tc; / Dr I. Everson 41cl / J. Foott 7bl, 35tr, 46br, 53b / F. Lanting 35cr / N. Lightfoot 53ca / D. & M. Plage 58b / Dr E. Potts 37cr / H. Reinhard: 43tl; R. Ellis 62bl; E.T. Archive 53tc; Mary Evans Picture Library 32tr, 34tl, 36bl, 37tl, 42cl, 48br, 50tl, 55bl, 63tr; FLPA - Images of nature: Frans Lanting/Minden Pictures 64br; Gerald Lacz 64cl; Minden Pictures 65bc, 71c. Werner Forman Archive / Field Museum of Natural History, USA 52cla; Greenpeace / Culley 49br / Gleizes 53cr / Martenson 59tl / Rowlands 59bl; © Hergé 9cr; Michael Holford 32bl, 56cl; I.F.A.W. 31cr; Jacana / F. Gohier 20cl, 21cr; Kendall Whaling Museum, Sharon ,Mass. / USA 50cl, 51clb; Frank Lane Picture Agency / T. Stephenson 63tl; Peter Lugårch 40cl; Mail Newspapers / Solo Syndication 63bl; Marineland / J. Foudraz 29tr, 29c; Minden Pictures / © F. Nicklin 39tr; Musée d'Histoire Naturelle, Paris / Gallimard Jeunesse 12bc; Natural History Museum, London 8tl, 9br, 10ca, 10cb, 20b, 36-37, 56cr, 70crb; NHPA / ANT 68tl; B. & C. Alexander 59tc / D. Currey 62tr / P. Johnson 29crb; / T Kitchen and V Hurst 71cl; / Stephen Krasemann 69cra; / T. Nakuniara 30cl; / Dave Watts 69br; O.S.F / D. Allan 18cl, 25b, 37tr, 37cra, 49tl, 58tl, 58tr, 63cr / D. Fleetham 26bl / L.E. Lauber 28cl / T. Martin 49tr; Oxford Scientific Films: Howard Hall 64cla; Pacific Whale Foundation / © 1990 D. Moses 57br; V. Papastavrou 12tl, 38br; Planet Earth Pictures / J. King 38bl / Menuhin 18tr / F. Schulke 60tr / M. Snyderman 20cr, 33clb / J. D. Watt 6cl; Rex Features Limited / E. Thorburn 27tr / Roger-Viollet 21tr; Ann Ronan at Image Select 47tl, 48tr; Courtesy of the Royal British Columbia Museum, Victoria, B.C., Canada / B. Reid 54tr; Science Photo Library / European Space Agency 39tl; Sea Life Cruises / R. Fairbairns 17c; Sea Mammal Research Unit, Cambridge / Dr C. Lockyer 61bl; C. Hunter 61crb / Dr T Martin 56tl, 60cr, 62br; Service Historique de la Marine, Vincennes / Gallimard Jeunesse 6bl; Frank Spooner Pictures / Gamma 58cl; S. Steedman 57cl; Texas A & M University at Galveston / Dr B. Würsig 32br; Wild Dolphin Project Inc. / D. Herzing 29tl, 31tl.

Jacket credits:
Museum of Natural History: back c.
Natural History Museum: back tl.
Town Docks Museum: back ca.
FLPA - Images of Nature: M Hoshino / Minden Pictures: front.